SALVATION

New Life in Christ

Study Guide

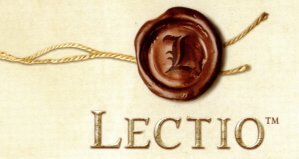

Unveiling Scripture and Tradition

MICHAEL PATRICK BARBER

Nihil Obstat: Currently under review.
Imprimatur:

Copyright © 2019 Augustine Institute. All rights reserved.
With the exception of short excerpts used in articles and critical reviews, no part of this work may be reproduced, transmitted, or stored in any form whatsoever, printed or electronic, without the prior permission of the publisher.

Scripture verses contained herein are from the Second Catholic Edition of the Revised Standard Version of the Bible, copyright ©1965, 1966 by the Division of Christian Educators of the National Council of the Churches of Christ in the United States of America. Used by permission. All rights reserved.

Excerpts from the English translation of the *Catechism of the Catholic Church*, Second Edition, © 1994, 1997, 2000 by Libreria Editrice Vaticana–United States Catholic Conference, Washington, D.C. All rights reserved.

Writers: Kimberly Barber, Sarah Christmyer, Ashley Crane, Kris Gray, Hannah Graves, Margaret Graves

Media: Steve Flanigan, Justin Leddick, Aurora Cerulli, Ryan Bradshaw, Ted Mast, Jon Ervin, Matthew Krekeler

Print Production/Graphic Design: Grace Hagan, Kirk Flory, Christina Gray, Ann Diaz, Milana del Río Tucker

Augustine Institute
6160 South Syracuse Way, Suite 310
Greenwood Village, CO 80111
Information: 303-937-4420
AugustineInstitute.org
Formed.org

Printed in the United States of America
ISBN 978-1-950939-11-4

TABLE OF CONTENTS

SALVATION
NEW LIFE IN CHRIST

Welcome to Lectio 5

Session 1: Not Self-Help 7

Session 2: Not Just Fire Insurance 27

Session 3: Not without Cost 49

Session 4: Not Just Personal 67

Session 5: Not Just a Legal Transaction 87

Session 6: Not a Spectator Sport 107

Session 7: Not Simply a Moment 127

Session 8: Not Inevitable 149

Session 9: Not Just for Other People 169

Session 10: Not Only about the Future 187

Lectio™

UNVEILING SCRIPTURE AND TRADITION

What Is Lectio?

To read is to discover meaning from written symbols or text. Letters form into words, words into sentences, and sentences into whole paragraphs and pages that communicate our thoughts, teach new ideas, and narrate stories that we find amusing, sorrowful, imaginative, or deeply profound.

The Latin term *lectio* means "reading." The tradition of reading Sacred Scripture for prayer and reflection was practiced by many of the early Church Fathers—St. Ambrose, St. Jerome, St. Augustine, St. Cyprian, and St. John Chrysostom, just to name a few. Benedictine monks later developed this practice into the tradition known as *lectio divina*, or "divine reading."

Lectio uses the practice of prayerful reading and study to help us dive more deeply into the truths of the Faith and discover the profound meaning and purpose of Sacred Scripture, Sacred Tradition, and Church History. We combine engaging sessions led by Catholic teachers with practical guidance for living the Faith and developing the disciplines of reading, reflecting, and responding.

By prayerfully reading and understanding the texts of Sacred Scripture and Tradition, we can come to discover the story of salvation into which our Baptism has united us, the history of God's people through the centuries, and the depth of God's love for each of us.

Welcome to Lectio

Welcome to the Lectio Study Series. In these study sessions of Lectio, you will discover the profound importance, meaning, purpose, and beauty of Sacred Scripture and Sacred Tradition, as seen through the eyes of the Church.

Lectio studies are designed for adult faith formation to help unveil both Sacred Scripture and Sacred Tradition. The Latin word *lectio* means "reading," and often refers to a careful and prayerful reading of Scripture. These studies cover a wide variety of topics, including individual books or letters of the Bible, the lives and writings of the saints, and Church teaching to help serve the formation of Catholics living out the call of the New Evangelization.

A Lectio Session

This Study Guide takes you step by step through each session, both the small group gathering and video teaching, as well as five days of personal follow-up study. The resources are carefully crafted to lead you through an opening of your heart and mind to God's Word and the Traditions of the Catholic Church.

What You'll Find in Each Lectio Session:

CONNECT

1. **Opening Prayer:** For this study on Salvation, the Opening Prayer for many of the sessions is taken from the Church's liturgical prayers celebrating the great hope of eternal unity with Christ.

2. **Introduction**: We begin with a brief overview of the topic, including the key points for the session. This helps contextualize the topic, show its relevance for daily life, and inspire you to delve into a particular aspect of the Faith.

3. **CONNECT Questions:** After reviewing the memory verse and daily reflections from the previous session, you'll share your thoughts on questions related to the new session.

VIDEO

4. **Video Teaching:** The video segments present teaching that delves into and makes relevant the Sacred Scripture and Sacred Tradition of the Catholic Church. The video teachings for the study on Salvation are presented by Michael Patrick Barber, Associate Professor of Sacred Scripture and Theology at the Augustine Institute. The Study Guide includes a brief outline of the key points in the teaching.

DISCUSS

5. **DISCUSS Questions:** Each video segment is followed by questions that will help you personalize and take ownership of the topics of the session.

6. **Memory Verse:** The participants are encouraged to memorize and reflect on a Scripture verse for every session so as to nurture the faith that has been deepened through your catechetical session.

7. **Closing Prayer:** The Closing Prayer has been chosen to reflect back to God an appropriate response to his loving action in the session.

8. **For Further Reading:** For supplemental study, you are encouraged to refer to the additional reading resources.

9. **Quotes, Tips, and Definitions**: We have included throughout the study interesting quotes and excerpts from saints, Catholic documents, the *Catechism of the Catholic Church*, and Catholic authors to enhance your understanding of each topic.

COMMIT

The Study Guide includes five daily COMMIT reflections that will help you more deeply explore the main topics of each session and more firmly commit to following Christ in your daily life. These reflections include more information on Sacred Tradition and Sacred Scripture, as well as topics such as geography, history, and art. Some of these reflections will also include times of prayer, including the practice of Scripture meditation known as *lectio divina*.

An Overview of Lectio Divina

Lectio divina is an ancient practice of enhancing one's prayer life through the power of God's Word. The term itself means "divine reading" of the Sacred Scriptures. It is our hope that by using these simple steps each day as you study Sacred Scripture in Lectio, you will develop an effective way to study and pray with God's Word and hear God's voice in your daily life.

- **Sacred Reading of the Scriptures (*lectio*):** The reading and rereading of the Scripture passage, paying close attention to words, details, themes, and patterns that speak to you.

- **Meditation (*meditatio*):** Meditating or reflecting on what you've read to gain understanding. Allow the Holy Spirit to guide you as you spend time pondering what you have read and striving to understand it in meditation.

- **Prayer (*oratio*):** A time to bring your meditative thoughts to God in prayer. Talking with God about how the connections and implications of your meditation on the Scripture affect your life and the lives of those around you.

- **Contemplation (*contemplatio*):** A time of quiet and rest, we listen and await God's voice. Contemplation allows one to enter decisively and more deeply into the mystery of God—this is no small endeavor, so be patient as you engage this step and strive to be receptive to God's voice speaking into your life.

- **Resolution (*resolutio*):** A call for resolution and action, inviting you to respond to the things you have read in Scripture and have prayed about and to put them into practice.

To learn more about *lectio divina*, refer to Dr. Tim Gray's Lectio: Prayer study, available at AugustineInstitute.org/programs, or his book *Praying Scripture for a Change*, available at www.AscensionPress.com.

SESSION 1

Not Self-Help

OPENING PRAYER

O God of unchanging power and eternal light,
look with favor on the wonderous mystery of the whole Church
and serenely accomplish the work of human salvation,
which you planned from all eternity;
may the whole world know and see
that what was cast down is raised up,
what had become old is made new,
and all things are restored to integrity through Christ,
just as by him they came into being.
Who lives and reigns for ever and ever.
Amen.
—Prayer after seventh reading, Easter Vigil

INTRODUCTION

Jesus came to earth to save us! We affirm that truth every time we say the Nicene Creed at Mass: he came down from Heaven "for our salvation." But what does that mean? In this first episode, Dr. Michael Barber explains why every Catholic should understand the importance of salvation: not just for our eternal state, but for our lives here and now. Drawing on Scripture and Tradition, he begins to discuss what it means to "be saved" and launches into the first of ten misconceptions that can lead to spiritual pitfalls: the idea that salvation is a matter of "self-help."

© Evdokimov Maxim/shutterstock.com

Connect

Introduce yourself to the group and share one thing you hope to get out of this class.

Has anyone ever asked you the question "Are you saved?" How did you respond? (Or if you haven't been asked, how do you think you would respond?)

Gift-giving is a source of joy, both for the giver and the receiver. To whom, and for what reasons, do we give and receive gifts? What effect does gift-giving have on a relationship?

Video

Watch the video segment. Use the outline below to follow along and take notes.

I. Salvation is central to our faith
   A. Jesus became man "for us men and our salvation" (Nicene Creed)
      1. Jesus named "for he will save his people from their sins" (Matthew 1:21)
      2. "Jesus" (*Yehoshua* in Hebrew) means "God saves" (see *CCC*, 430)
   B. How to answer: what does it mean to "be saved"?
      1. Start with Scripture, which is "the soul of sacred theology" (*Dei Verbum*, 24)
      2. In context of Tradition; "Tradition means giving votes to the most obscure of all classes, our ancestors." (G.K. Chesterton, *Orthodoxy*)
      3. Right understanding impacts life and discipleship
II. Misconception: Salvation as self-help
   A. Paul links new life to grace
      1. Greek *charis* means "gift"
      2. "For by grace you have been saved . . . it is the gift of God" (Ephesians 2:8)
   B. Gift-giving in ancient Greco-Roman society

SESSION 1

NOT SELF-HELP

- C. What is grace?
    1. Jesus "gave himself for our sins" (Galatians 1:4)
    2. The gift is a person: Jesus Christ
    3. Jesus continually gives himself to believers
- D. God gives his gift to the unworthy
    1. "Christ died for the ungodly" (Romans 5:6)
    2. Jesus comes to save *and* to seek (Zacchaeus in Luke 19)
    3. Jesus comes because he knows we are unworthy!
    4. Salvation only possible because of grace (*CCC*, 2010; John 15:5)

DISCUSS

1. What one thing do you want to remember from what you heard in the teaching?

2. Based on what you heard in the video, why is it important to know what it means to be saved?

3. What does it mean to think of salvation as "self-help"? Have you ever thought of salvation that way, or do you know someone who does? According to Dr. Barber, why is this a dangerous misconception?

SESSION 1   NOT SELF-HELP

4. Dr. Barber explains that "grace" (*charis*) was a common term in Greco-Roman culture, meaning "gift." How is gift-giving and its intent in Paul's day like or unlike the way it is perceived today? What is countercultural about God's gift of grace?

___

5. In what way is living as though salvation is self-help rejecting the Gospel? What are ways you have found or might use to overcome that temptation?

___

Quotes, Tips, & Definitions

Grace is the gift of the Son, who gave himself on the Cross and who dwells in us so we can live a new life and become like the Giver.

—Dr. Michael Barber

Grace is favor, the free and undeserved help that God gives us to respond to his call to become children of God, adoptive sons, partakers of the divine nature and of eternal life.

—Catechism of the Catholic Church, 1996

MEMORY VERSE

For by grace you have been saved through faith; and this is not your own doing, it is the gift of God.

—Ephesians 2:8

CLOSING PRAYER

Blessed be the Lord, the God of Israel;
he has come to his people and set them free.
He has raised up for us a mighty savior . . . .

This was the oath he swore to our father Abraham:
to set us free from the hands of our enemies,
free to worship him without fear,
holy and righteous in his sight all the days of our life . . . .

© shutterstock.com

In the tender compassion of our God
the dawn from on high shall break upon us,
to shine on those who dwell in darkness and the shadow of death,
and to guide our feet into the way of peace.

Glory to the Father, and to the Son, and to the Holy Spirit,
as it was in the beginning, is now, and will be for ever. Amen.

—Canticle of Zechariah (see Luke 1:68–79)

FOR FURTHER READING

John M. G. Barclay, *Paul and the Gift* (Grand Rapids: Eerdmans, 2015)

Catechism of the Catholic Church, 1987–2029 ("Grace and Justification")

Placuit Deo, "Letter to the Bishops of the Catholic Church on Certain Aspects of Christian Salvation," 2018

Commit—Day 1
Grace as God's Merciful Gift

For by grace you have been saved through faith; and this is not your own doing, it is the gift of God.

—Ephesians 2:8

© Linda Bucklin/shutterstock.com

Many today feel that the important thing is to be "spiritual" and not "religious"—a difference that often means throwing out rules (not to mention uncomfortable concepts like sin and Hell) and seeking simply a feeling of communion with the divine. Pope Francis has spoken and written about this at length, and in 2018 the Holy See issued a letter to bishops about the cultural shifts that make it hard to understand certain aspects of salvation. According to *Placuit Deo*,

> *A new form of Pelagianism is spreading in our days, one in which the individual ... presumes to save oneself, without recognizing that, at the deepest level of being, he or she derives from God and from others. According to this way of thinking, salvation depends on the strength of the individual or on purely human structures, which are incapable of welcoming the newness of the Spirit of God. (Placuit Deo, 4)*

This attitude contributes to the first misconception Dr. Barber tackles in this series: that salvation is about "self-help" and is something we achieve on our own.

Have you seen this attitude in your life or in those you know? When or how?

_____

_____

_____

_____

© Sergey Tinyakov/shutterstock.com

SESSION 1 NOT SELF-HELP

Anyone striving to save himself is bound to hit their limitations at some point. How does St. Paul describe the problem in Romans 7:19–20? What does he say is the cause of it?

_____

_____

_____

CONCUPISCENCE: The Inclination to Sin

Yet certain temporal consequences of sin remain in the baptized, such as suffering, illness, death, and such frailties inherent in life as weaknesses of character, and so on, as well as an inclination to sin that Tradition calls concupiscence . . . since concupiscence "is left for us to wrestle with, it cannot harm those who do not consent but manfully resist it by the grace of Jesus Christ."

—*Catechism of the Catholic Church*, 1264

Perhaps you have felt this in yourself and can relate to Paul's words when he continues in verse 24, "Wretched man that I am! Who will deliver me from this body of death?" There is only one answer: God and his gift of grace.

God knows us better than we know ourselves. He knows we will tend to swing between the poles of determined self-sufficiency on one hand and despair over our weakness on the other. In his mercy, he gives us everything we need. We have only to humble ourselves and receive the gift of his grace, like little children putting our hands in the hand of a loving father. As St. Elizabeth Ann Seton wrote, "We know certainly that our God calls us to a holy life, that He gives us every grace, every abundant grace; and though we are so weak of ourselves, this grace is able to carry us through every obstacle and difficulty."

In the earliest days of the Church, St. Paul wrote a letter to Titus. The young man was in charge of building the fledgling church in Crete, with the task of promoting both right understanding and practice of the Faith, something Paul called "knowledge of the truth which accords with godliness" (Titus 1:1). As a bishop, it was important that Titus be blameless and a model of good works among a people who "profess to know God, but they deny him by their deeds; they are detestable, disobedient, unfit for any good deed" (Titus 1:16). In short, they needed the gift of grace! Titus is to rebuke and teach. Perhaps Paul foresaw the possibility of a "self-help" misconception by which people might attempt to "clean up their act" on their own power, and so Paul makes clear the primary role of grace in salvation and good works.

SESSION 1

Read Titus 2:11–14. What is the primary reason God's grace has appeared, and for whom? What are its effects?

_____
_____
_____

Recall that "grace" *(charis)* means "gift." What gift is described here?

_____
_____
_____

What do the following verses add to your understanding of grace as a gift?

Romans 6:23: _____

Galatians 1:3–4: _____

In closing, spend a few minutes reflecting on the free gift of grace that God has given you. Thank him for it and ask for help to give up any tendency to strive for salvation through self-help so that you can receive the fullness of his gift.

_____
_____
_____

© BrankaVV/shutterstock.com

There is no struggle to earn or merit God's gift. All is given gratuitously and in its time. The Lord gives to all gratuitously. Salvation isn't purchased, it's not paid for: it's a free gift.

—Pope Francis,
General Audience May 29, 2019

Commit—Day 2
Saving Faith as a Gift

One thing that becomes clear as we read these Scriptures about God's gift of grace is that Jesus does not save us for the reason that we are "worth it." We aren't! Nor does he save us for the reason that we "deserve it." We don't! St. Paul is clear that Jesus died specifically for the ungodly (see Romans 5:6). God desires to save us because he loves us. Our failures and weaknesses simply manifest, in all its glory, the riches of the grace God has lavished upon us (see Ephesians 2:7).

Even our love for God and the faith with which we respond to him comes to us from God. As Paul wrote to the Ephesians, "[B]y grace you have been saved through faith; and *this is not your own doing, it is the gift of God*—not because of works, lest any man should boast" (Ephesians 2:8–9, emphasis added). It is always God who moves first.

Faith is the act of the intellect when it assents to divine truth under the influence of the will moved by God through grace.
—St. Thomas Aquinas, *Summa Theologica*, II.II.q2.a.9

One of the pitfalls of presuming on salvation by self-help is the tendency toward prideful boasting. Jesus spoke to this in a parable he told to people whose trust in their own righteousness made them look down on others.

© Morphart Creation/shutterstock.com

SESSION 1

NOT SELF-HELP

Read the parable in Luke 18:9–14. Describe the Pharisee and his prayer. How many times does the Pharisee refer to himself in his prayer? What does that tell you?

_____
_____
_____

The Pharisee presents himself as one who even goes beyond what is required by law, fasting twice a week and tithing on everything he gets. According to Jesus in Matthew 22:36–40, on what commandments does the whole law depend? How does the Pharisee measure up to them?

_____
_____
_____

Now describe the tax collector's prayer.

_____
_____
_____

What does Jesus conclude about the two men?

_____
_____
_____

JUSTIFICATION

As an action, justification is the moment when God makes righteous the one who believes in Christ and establishes him or her in a covenant relationship with himself. As a process, justification is the growth in righteousness and grace that takes place in the believer who embraces the demands of the gospel and yields himself or herself to the leading of the Spirit.

In reference to the [tax collector and Pharisee of Luke 18], . . . The lesson is that justification consists in the mercy of God that is given graciously to sinners who acknowledge their guilt but is withheld from those who consider themselves righteous because of their outward piety.

—*Catholic Bible Dictionary*, Scott Hahn, General Editor, pgs. 496, 497

It might seem counterintuitive that becoming aware of your sin and inadequacy is a prerequisite to being saved. This awareness can be humiliating. But it is precisely this recognition of our own unworthiness and our extraordinary need that frees us from our pride so that we put our trust and faith in the only one who can save us: the Lord.

> *We must not think Pride is something God forbids because He is offended at it, or that Humility is something He demands as due to His own dignity—as if God Himself was proud. He is not in the least worried about His dignity. The point is, He wants you to know Him: wants to give you Himself. And He and you are two things of such a kind that if you really get into any kind of touch with Him you will, in fact, be humble—delightedly humble, feeling the infinite relief of having for once got rid of all the silly nonsense about your own dignity which has made you restless and unhappy all your life. He is trying to make you humble in order to make this moment possible: trying to take off a lot of silly, ugly, fancy-dress in which we have all got ourselves up and are strutting about like the little idiots we are.*
>
> —C. S. Lewis, *Mere Christianity*

Humility frees us to beat our breast like the tax collector, or to fall to our knees before Jesus like Peter in his boat and proclaim, "Depart from me, for I am a sinful man, O Lord" (Luke 5:8). Only in this lowly state can we hear Jesus say to us, "Do not be afraid," and have the courage to put our faith and trust in the unmerited gift of God. If you lack that faith, remember it comes from God; you have only to ask. Like the father who can't quite believe Jesus will heal his son in Mark 9:24, you can pray to the Lord, "I believe; help my unbelief!"

Mary, "full of grace," expressed perfectly the humility that is the opposite of "salvation by self-help" and that is the foundation of saving faith. Her Magnificat is a fitting response to Jesus's parable of the Pharisee and the tax collector. Read Luke 1:46–54 prayerfully. What stands out to you? Ask the Blessed Mother to help you humbly seek the Lord and his grace.

© Bogdan Vasilescu/shutterstock.com

Commit—Day 3

Lectio: Zacchaeus

Any visitor to Rome who has arrived early to St. Peter's Square and fought their way to a front-row seat for the Pope's Wednesday audience can relate to Zacchaeus, the short publican who climbed a tree to see Jesus as he passed. People stand on chairs, climb on shoulders, *anything* to get a glimpse of the Holy Father. And if he happens to look your way or (wonder of wonders!) reach out and grasp your hand—it's a story to be retold for generations. Today's *lectio* reflection takes us into the story of Zacchaeus and considers how it is not only we who seek Jesus, but Jesus who himself comes "to seek and to save" the lost.

> **Lectio:** The practice of praying with Scripture, *lectio divina* begins with an active and close reading of the Scripture passage. Read the verse below and then answer the questions to take a closer look at some of the details of the passage.

[Jesus] entered Jericho and was passing through. And there was a man named Zacchae'us; he was a chief tax collector, and rich. And he sought to see who Jesus was, but could not, on account of the crowd, because he was small of stature. So he ran on ahead and climbed up into a sycamore tree to see him, for he was to pass that way. And when Jesus came to the place, he looked up and said to him, "Zacchae'us, make haste and come down; for I must stay at your house today." So he made haste and came down, and received him joyfully. And when they saw it they all murmured, "He has gone in to be the guest of a man who is a sinner." And Zacchae'us stood and said to the Lord, "Behold, Lord, the half of my goods I give to the poor; and if I have defrauded any one of anything, I restore it fourfold." And Jesus said to him, "Today salvation has come to this house, since he also is a son of Abraham. For the Son of man came to seek and to save the lost."

—Luke 19:1–10

Circle all the verbs used to describe Zacchaeus's actions, with any associated adverbs (verbs are usually action words; adverbs describe that action further: "looked carefully," for example). What do these words reveal about Zacchaeus?

_____

_____

_____

SESSION 1

NOT SELF-HELP

Underline the opening sentence and what Jesus first says to Zacchaeus and compare them, writing down any contrast you see. What might be responsible for the difference?

_____
_____
_____

As a tax collector, Zacchaeus is a known collaborator with the Roman occupation forces, and his wealth would have been gained by cheating his fellow Jews. Describe the different reactions of the crowd and Zacchaeus to Jesus's decision to dine in Zacchaeus's house. What is Jesus's response to Zacchaeus's promise?

_____
_____
_____

> **MEDITATIO:** *Lectio*, a close reading and rereading of Scripture, is followed by *meditatio*, a time to reflect on the Scripture passage and to ponder the reason for particular events, descriptions, details, phrases, and even echoes from other Scripture passages that were noticed during *lectio*. Take some time now to meditate on the above verse.

God excludes no one, neither the poor nor the rich. God does not let himself be conditioned by our human prejudices, but sees in everyone a soul to save and is especially attracted to those who are judged as lost and who think themselves so. Jesus Christ, the Incarnation of God, has demonstrated this immense mercy, which takes nothing away from the gravity of sin, but aims always at saving the sinner, at offering him the possibility of redemption, of starting again from the beginning, of converting. In another passage of the Gospel Jesus states that it is very difficult for a rich man to enter the Kingdom of Heaven (cf. Mt 19:23). In the case of Zacchaeus we see that precisely what seems impossible actually happens: "He", St Jerome comments, "gave away his wealth and immediately replaced it with the wealth of the Kingdom of Heaven" (Homily on Psalm 83:3). [. . .] Dear Friends, Zacchaeus welcomed Jesus and he converted because Jesus first welcomed him! He did not condemn him but he met his desire for salvation.

—Pope Benedict XVI, Sunday Angelus, October 31, 2010

SESSION 1

Not Self-Help

Jesus demonstrated God's mercy over and over again during his life on earth, as is shown in the following verses. Who are the "lost" that he reaches out to in each instance?

Matthew 8:2–4: _____

Matthew 8:5–13: _____

Mark 1:23–27: _____

Mark 2:15–17: _____

Luke 6:20–22: _____

John 8:3–11: _____

In this story of Zacchaeus, what does Jesus mean that he came not just to save but to seek the lost?

_____

_____

_____

Zakæ (Christ and Zacchaeus), Niels Larsen Stevns
© Gunnar Bach Pedersen, Randers Museum of Art, Randers, Denmark

SESSION 1 NOT SELF-HELP

Like the people you have just read about, do you ever feel lost or excluded by society or even by other Christians? Is there something in your past or present that keeps you from full communion or because of which you avoid Jesus's presence? Or is there someone *you* exclude because you don't think they belong? Read again the story of Zacchaeus, putting yourself in the scene. How does it apply to your situation? Ask Jesus to speak to you through his Word. Write what you hear.

_____
_____
_____

Jesus seeks out Zacchaeus, or as Pope Benedict says, "Jesus first welcomed him!" Jesus asks Zacchaeus to "make haste and come down" so he can spend time with him at his house. Is there some way that Jesus is welcoming and inviting you to "come down" from your "tree"—to turn away from sin, or to leave a place where you are observing him, but not interacting? Make haste! What is he inviting you to today?

_____
_____
_____

We must not think that it is the sinner, through his own independent journey of conversion, who earns mercy. On the contrary, it is mercy that impels him along the path of conversion. Left to himself, man can do nothing and he deserves nothing. Before being man's journey to God, confession is God's arrival at a person's home.
—St. John Paul II, Letter of the Holy Father to Priests for Holy Thursday 2002

> **ORATIO, CONTEMPLATIO, RESOLUTIO:** Having read and meditated on today's Scripture passage, take some time to pray, to bring your thoughts to God (*oratio*), and to be receptive to God's grace in silence (*contemplatio*). Then end your prayer by making a simple concrete resolution (*resolutio*) to respond to God's prompting of your heart in today's prayer.

_____
_____
_____

Commit—Day 4
Returning to the Father

We began this session by identifying the misconception of salvation as self-help, and we learned that salvation is not about becoming a "better you" and thus working your way into Heaven. Salvation, rather, is something that is given as a gift and made possible by God's grace, his gift of himself in the person of his Son. Ultimately, what that does is to bring us back to the Father as sons and daughters ourselves. We don't just obtain a pass to give St. Peter when we meet him at the pearly gates. Rather, we are transformed here and now to be like Christ (and love others like the children of God that we are) here on earth.

Because of the Fall, we are continually tempted to forget the love and grace of God. Self-help is about denying God's help. Instead of resting in the arms of our heavenly Father and relying on him, we can picture ourselves called before him as though he's a hostile judge who is barring our way to happiness. And if we think it's up to us to earn our way into his good graces, we can swing between despair over ever being good enough on one hand, and resentment on the other.

The Return of the Prodigal Son, Zvonimir Atletic
© shutterstock.com

The pitfalls of despair and resentment are illustrated by the two sons in Jesus's parable of the prodigal son in Luke 15:11–32 (or the parable of the merciful father, as it might be called). The younger son takes the father's gift of an early inheritance and runs away to spend it on himself. When it is gone and he is glad to eat even the slop left out for the pigs, he finds "no one gave him anything" (Luke 15:16). He has fallen so far that he can't imagine his father would accept him back as a son. He knows that his father's servants are treated better than he is, though, so he determines to return, repent, and settle into a life of cared-for servitude.

The older son also received the gift of early inheritance (see verse 12, where the father literally divided his "life"—*bios* in the Greek—between them). Everything his father has is his, but he doesn't appreciate it. If the younger son fell into servitude, the older son sought it out. Everything he has done on the family farm—on the property that is *his*—he sees as slavish, unrewarded work for a man he won't even call "father." Neither does he call the other son "brother." He has left his father as certainly as his younger brother did, even though he never left home.

SESSION 1

NOT SELF-HELP

Take a moment to read Luke 15:11–32. Do you identify with either of the sons? Which one and how?

_____

_____

_____

The focus of the parable is on the father. It is a similar story to the two parables that precede it in Luke 15: the parable of the lost sheep and the parable of the lost coin. Both of those highlight the heavenly joy that greets any person, however small or unimportant, who repents. The father's aim is not to punish but to receive back into his family those who have left or rejected him or lost their way. He seeks them out in love. He reinstates them in the family. But he doesn't ignore their sin. The younger son abandons his self-seeking pleasures and humbly returns. That he "came to himself" (Luke 15:17) is a sign of his repentance. He returns to receive the full family status he did not expect or deserve (symbolized by the gifts he receives: the robe and ring and shoes). In contrast, the older son's case is left open-ended. He is invited to cast off his sour resentment, forgive his brother, and celebrate his return. But will he go in? The hearer is left to imagine himself or herself in the older brother's shoes.

The Return of the Prodigal Son, James Tissot
©wikiart.org

If you identify with the older son, how do you respond to God's invitation to the grace of his gift?

_____

_____

_____

In closing, consider once again Paul's words to the Ephesians: "By grace you have been saved through faith; and this is not your own doing, it is the gift of God—not because of works, lest any man should boast" (Ephesians 2:8–9). Our loving heavenly Father will never abandon you. Should you lose your way, he will seek you out. He takes the initiative to save you by the gift of his Son. Spend a few moments in prayer, thanking God for his precious and wonderful gift.

COMMIT–DAY 5
TRUTH AND BEAUTY

Return of the Prodigal Son
by Bartolome Esteban Murillo, 1667/1670, National Gallery

Return of the Prodigal Son, Bartolome Esteban Murillo
© wikiart

In the 1660s the Spanish painter Bartolome Esteban Murillo created a series of paintings on the parable of the prodigal son (Luke 15:11–32), each portraying various moments in the story, including the prodigal's departure, his feasting, his being thrown out into the streets after he had squandered all his money, his being reduced to a slave feeding the swine, and finally the prodigal's return. Murillo returned to the subject of the prodigal son's return when, around 1670, he produced the enormous work, measuring roughly eight feet by eight feet, that is the subject of today's reflection.

In this *Return of the Prodigal Son,* Murillo puts before us the climactic moment when the returning prodigal encounters his father. The rags that the prodigal wears—a shirt so torn that the son's shoulder is no longer covered, and pants so worn that they barely resemble shorts—and the dirty soles of his unshod feet recall the dire situation into which the prodigal has been reduced because of his self-indulgent ways. The prodigal's folded hands are drawn into his breast and his pleading face recalls the rehearsed words he speaks to his father.

SESSION 1   NOT SELF-HELP

Look up the following verses. What did the prodigal intend to say to his father? And what portion of this is he unable to proclaim?

In Luke 15:17–19, he intends to say: _____

_____

In Luke 15:21, he says: _____

_____

Before he can finish speaking, the father draws his wayward son into his arms. One of the moving aspects of this painting is how the father, dressed in his voluminous, rich robe, fills the center of the painting. At the prodigal's repentance, he is enveloped into his father's loving embrace and now shares the center of the painting with the father, a vivid image of the joyful restoration that is taking place out of the father's compassion.

Look up the following verses. What commands does the father give to his servants?

Luke 15:22–23: _____

_____

In the painting, the father's commands to his servants are already put into motion as servants flank the father and son from the right and left. On the right, household servants bring a tray piled high with a rich new robe and sandals. Another servant holds up the ring that is to be placed on the prodigal's finger. On the left, a laborer bestows a loving glance on his son as he leads the fatted calf for the feast so that all can make merry and rejoice at the prodigal's return.

The muted buildings and clouds of the background keep the viewer's attention on the interactions of the foreground. The various facial expressions fill the painting with emotion, from the central expression of the father and prodigal son, to the wonder of the servant holding the ring, or the cheerful grin on the young boy. Even the excited leap of the family dog as it greets its long-lost owner adds to the anticipation of the feast that is about to take place.

This painting was one of six large paintings Murillo produced for the chapel of the Charity Hospital of Seville, a hospice for the homeless and hungry run by the Brotherhood of Charity, one of Seville's major lay confraternities. Originally focused on providing a proper burial for the poor, the confraternity expanded their charitable works to include care for the sick. Each of Murillo's paintings presented one of the seven works of mercy (the seventh, burying of the dead, was done as a sculpture by another artist). The *Return of the Prodigal Son* focused on the clothing of the naked. These enormous paintings hung on the walls of the chapel, gorgeously depicting biblical scenes of God's mercy and directing both patient and caregiver alike to meditation on the loving care of the Divine Physician, Jesus Christ.

SESSION 1

Take a moment to journal your ideas, questions, or insights about this session. Write down thoughts you had that may not have been mentioned in the text or the discussion questions. List any personal applications you got from the lessons. What challenged you the most in the teachings? How might you turn what you've learned into specific action?

SESSION 2

NOT JUST FIRE INSURANCE

OPENING PRAYER

O God, supreme Father of the faithful,
who increases the children of your promise
by pouring out the grace of adoption
throughout the whole world
and who through the Paschal Mystery
make your servant Abraham father of nations,
as once you swore,
grant, we pray,
that your peoples may enter worthily
into the grace to which you call them.
Through Christ our Lord.
Amen.
—Prayer after second reading, Easter Vigil

INTRODUCTION

"Salvation as self-help" is only the first of many common misunderstandings that can become pitfalls in the way we understand and live our faith. In this session, Dr. Barber addresses the common misconception that salvation is like "fire insurance": that it's all about saving people from the fires of Hell. Jesus doesn't simply save us *from* Hell; he also saves us *for* something wonderful: "abundant life." Dr. Barber explains how a proper understanding of the Old Testament concepts of law and covenant reveals the essential link between God's law and our happiness and fulfillment.

© grace21/shutterstock.com

Connect

What was your chief takeaway about salvation from last week's session? Did you have a preconception that was changed?

Have you known someone who views Catholicism primarily as a list of do's and don'ts? What impact does or did that have on their faith or the way they practice it?

In what way might salvation be considered a kind of "fire insurance"?

Video

Watch the video segment. Use the outline below to follow along and take notes.

I. Old Testament: The idea of life is central to law
   A. Torah: God's law is ordered to life
      1. Precepts give life (Psalm 119:13)
      2. Commands = "the law of life and knowledge" (Sirach 45:5)
   B. Law is linked to covenant
      1. Law as "the book of the covenant of . . . God" (Sirach 24:23)
      2. Covenant makes family bonds
      3. Covenant is ordered to love ("I am yours, you are mine")
      4. God's law is fatherly wisdom (see Baruch 3:9)

II. New Testament: Life is found in the law of love
   A. Jesus links commands to life
      1. For eternal life, keep commands (Matthew 19:16–17)
      2. A "new" command? (John 13:34 vs. Matthew 22:36–40; Leviticus 19:18)
      3. Not "as yourself" but "as I have loved you"
      4. Love fulfills the law (Romans 13:8–10)

SESSION 2

NOT JUST FIRE INSURANCE

  B. We are called to love *like* Christ and *with* Christ
    1. Salvation: communion with God who wants to dwell in us (see John 14:23)
    2. The gift: Christ "loved me and gave himself for me" (Galatians 2:20)
III. Only grace makes Christ-like love possible
  A. With God all things are possible (Matthew 19:26)
  B. Those who love, know God (1 John 4:7–8)
    1. "You only" = special (Amos 3:2)
    2. "Face to face" = relational (Deuteronomy 34)
    3. "I formed you in the womb" = intimate (Jeremiah 1:5)
  C. Greek term for this intimate relationship: *koinonia*
    1. Literally "fellowship," more apt "communion"
    2. Eternal life made manifest in Christ for *koinonia* (see 1 John 1:1–3)
    3. God's promise: escape corruption, partake in his nature (see 2 Peter 1:3–4)
    4. Christ's love leads to salvation, abundant life (see John 10:7–10, 14)

DISCUSS

1. What is the most important thing you heard in Dr. Barber's teaching?

SESSION 2

2. What did Dr. Barber mean when he said that the law of God is ultimately "the law of life"?

   _____
   _____
   _____

3. In the Old Testament, the greatest commands were to love God and neighbor. What is "new" about Jesus's "new" command?

   _____
   _____
   _____

4. What makes that level of love possible for us?

   _____
   _____
   _____

MEMORY VERSE

The thief comes only to steal and kill and destroy; I came that they may have life, and have it abundantly.

—John 10:10

Quotes, Tips, & Definitions

Salvation is not just about being forgiven of sins or being acquitted by a judge. Salvation is about communion with God himself.

—Dr. Michael Barber

CLOSING PRAYER

O God, who in the abasement of your Son have raised up a fallen world, fill your faithful with holy joy, for on those you have rescued from slavery to sin you bestow eternal gladness. Through our Lord Jesus Christ, your Son, who lives and reigns with you in the unity of the Holy Spirit, one God, for ever and ever. Amen.

—Collect, Wednesday of the Fourteenth Week of Ordinary Time

FOR FURTHER READING

Catechism of the Catholic Church, 1950–1986 ("Law and Grace")

Deus Caritas Est, Encyclical on Christian Love by Pope Benedict XVI, 2005

Scott Hahn, *A Father Who Keeps His Promises* (Cincinnati: Servant, 1998)

Peter Kreeft, *The God Who Loves You* (San Francisco: Ignatius Press, 2004)

Commit—Day 1
The Law and the Love of God

To many people, God seems all about law, as a cosmic judge who tallies up sins and sends to Hell those who go too far. With that kind of view, who wouldn't want "fire insurance"? Fortunately, though, God is not someone eagerly waiting to condemn people. As the Lord himself reminds the prophet Ezekiel, "As I live, says the Lord GOD, I have no pleasure in the death of the wicked" (Ezekiel 33:11). While Hell is real, and eternal damnation is a real possibility for those who turn away from God, God "desires all men to be saved" (1 Timothy 2:4). And by "saved," he doesn't only mean saved *from* Hell, he means saved *for* something wonderful. As Jesus said in John 10:10, "I came that they may have life, and have it abundantly."

The Entry of the Animals into Noah's Ark, Jacopo Bassano
© wikiart.org

Before we take a closer look at how we know this, and at what law, which is often seen as restrictive, has to do with life, take a minute to think about the phrase "abundant life." What does that mean to you?

_____

_____

_____

Even in the opening book of the Old Testament, the Bible demonstrates salvation as something more than fire insurance—or in this case, flood insurance—as early as Genesis 6–9, in the story of Noah and the Ark. At that time, "the LORD saw that the wickedness of man was great in the earth, and that every imagination of the thoughts of his heart was only evil continually" (Genesis 6:5). God saved the righteous man Noah and his family from that immoral cesspool and from the flood that washed it away.

At the same time, God saved Noah and his family for abundant life on the earth. "[B]e fruitful and multiply, bring forth abundantly on the earth and multiply in it," he commanded Noah in Genesis 9:7, promising to never destroy everything with a flood again and entering into a covenant with Noah and his descendants and all living animals. That covenant established a relationship between God and mankind based on God's promised support. It also included simple rules for life: be fruitful and don't eat the blood of animals or shed the blood of man.

SESSION 2

NOT JUST FIRE INSURANCE

COVENANT

A solemn agreement between human beings or between God and a human being involving mutual commitments or guarantees.

—*Catechism of the Catholic Church,* Glossary

Fast-forward ten generations and we see that God made another covenant to foster abundant life and help people thrive. This time, God called Abraham to leave everything behind and travel to a new land where he would be blessed beyond imagining. Abraham obeyed and, over time, God made "an everlasting covenant" with him, promising him countless descendants, land, and to bless them and the world through them (see Genesis 12:1–3 and Genesis 15, 17, and 22).

The people of Israel (Abraham's descendants through his son Isaac and grandson Jacob) were the recipients of God's next great saving act after they became slaves in Egypt. Once again, God not only saved his people *from* bondage, he also freed them *for* a covenant relationship with him, which was established on Mount Sinai. If anyone thinks that relationship was one of master to slave, they don't know the story.

Read Exodus 4:22. What is the relationship between God and Israel?

_____
_____

Now read Deuteronomy 7:7. Why did God choose Israel for this special relationship?

_____
_____

According to Deuteronomy 7:12–13, what do God's commands have to do with his covenant and abundant life?

_____
_____

. . . a covenant implies an adoption into the household, an extension of kinship, the making of a brother.

—Paul Kalluveettil, *Declaration and Covenant*

God does not give his commands or laws randomly. In Scripture we see that they are always given in the context of God's fatherly love and his covenant. Thus, with Noah, it is only after God has saved Noah and his family from the Flood and is entering into a covenant with Noah that he gives the commands not to eat the blood of animals or shed the blood of man.

So too at the time of the Exodus. Only after God's mighty wonders have saved his people from slavery in Egypt, and as they enter into a covenant relationship, does God give the Ten Commandments. Thus before the list of the Ten Commandments is given in Exodus 20:3–17, God reminds the people of his love that has set them free: "I am the Lord your God, who brought you out of the land of Egypt, out of the house of bondage" (Exodus 20:2).

© jorisvo/shutterstock.com

God's love is such that he wants the best for his people, and his laws help them live in a way that promotes their well-being. Because of this, God's law is not onerous, but life-giving. The Ten Commandments "express the implications of belonging to God through the establishment of the covenant. Moral existence is a *response* to the Lord's loving initiative. It is the acknowledgement and homage given to God and a worship of thanksgiving. It is cooperation with the plan God pursues in history" (*CCC*, 2062). Our fidelity to God's commands is a response of thanksgiving to God's love and all he has already done for us.

The saving events of the Flood and the Exodus, and the covenant relationship that was born out of them between God and his people, prefigured what Christ would do in the New Covenant. Just like Noah and the children of Israel were saved from corruption and slavery through water to become God's family, so we are saved from the corruption and slavery of sin through the water of Baptism to become children of God. As the Ten Commandments taught Israel to live as his free children after years of slavery, God's Word and his commands tell us how to live "like him"—in the image of the One who loves us and gave himself for us.

Think of your life as part of the story of salvation, a continuation of the narrative that reveals God's love for his people. Describe one way that God's law has meant life to you or shown his love.

_____

_____

Commit – Day 2
Fulfilling the Law

If it is indeed true that God created us for abundant life, and that he gives his law within the context of a covenant (permanent, loving, family) promise of blessing, then following that law by obeying its commands is what will lead to our greatest fulfillment!

The Ten Commandments are not an arbitrary imposition of a tyrannical Lord. [. . .] They save man from the destructive force of egoism, hatred and falsehood. They point out all the false gods that draw him into slavery: the love of self to the exclusion of God, the greed for power and pleasure that overturns the order of justice and degrades our human dignity and that of our neighbour. [. . .] To keep the Commandments is be faithful to God, but it is also to be faithful to ourselves, to our true nature and our deepest aspirations.
—**St. John Paul II, Celebration of the Word at Mount Sinai, February 26, 2000**

A generation after God freed them from Egypt, Joshua prepared to lead Israel into the Promised Land. What does Joshua 1:6–8 say about knowing and keeping God's law?

_____
_____
_____

What do the following verses call God's law?

Baruch 3:9: _____

Sirach 17:11: _____

SESSION 2 — NOT JUST FIRE INSURANCE

LAW

A rule of conduct established by competent authority for the common good. In biblical terms, the moral *law is the fatherly instruction of God, setting forth the ways which lead to happiness and proscribing those which lead to evil. The* divine *or* eternal *law can be either* natural *or* revealed *(positive). Natural moral law is inscribed in the heart, and known by human reason. Revealed law is found in the* ancient *law (Old Testament), notably the ten commandments, and in the* new *law (Law of the Gospel), the teaching of Christ, notably the Sermon on the Mount, which perfects the ancient law (1950–1974).*
—*Catechism of the Catholic Church*, Glossary

If it is God's law that gives wisdom and understanding and leads to life, it follows that *not* following that law (i.e., sinning) will lead away from life and, eventually, to death. Still, we can be tempted to think we know better than God does what is good for us, and that going our own way instead of his will bring happiness. True, there are times when doing something against God's law will bring pleasure; but that pleasure will be short-lived, and the ultimate result will tend toward the opposite. For that reason, Sirach 21:2 warns, "Flee from sin as from a snake; for if you approach sin, it will bite you. Its teeth are lion's teeth, and destroy the souls of men."

Psalm 19 juxtaposes the life-giving "word" or message of God that is evident in nature, particularly in the light and warmth of the sun, with the "light" that comes through the law of the Lord. In just three verses, Psalm 19 uses six different words for "law" along with descriptions that get across its nature and benefits. Fill in the following chart to show what those are. One of them is filled in for you.

Vs #: Word for "Law"	What It Is	What It Does
8a: Law		
8b: Decrees		
9a: Precepts		
9b: Commandment		
10a: Fear of the Lord (the way one reveres God, presumably by obeying the law)	Clean	Endures forever
10b: *Ordinances*		

Now read verses 10–11. What else does the psalmist say is true about God's laws?

© Boris Diakovsky/shutterstock.com

Psalm 1 provides a vivid picture of the abundant life that is the result of delighting in, meditating on, and following the law of the Lord. Describe that life.

Read John 15:1–17, which provides a New Testament parallel to this concept. From verses 1–5 and 8, describe briefly the parallel and what it tells you about how to have abundant life.

From John 15:9–11, what is the relationship between abiding and love, and between following the law and being fulfilled?

Does this reflect your own experience? Why or why not?

___

Since God is love and his law springs from his love for us and desire for our good, it's no wonder that the ultimate way to fulfill the law is to love. As Paul wrote in Romans 13:8–10:

> *Owe no one anything, except to love one another; for he who loves his neighbor has fulfilled the law. The commandments, "You shall not commit adultery, You shall not kill, You shall not steal, You shall not covet," and any other commandment, are summed up in this sentence, "You shall love your neighbor as yourself." Love does no wrong to a neighbor; therefore love is the fulfilling of the law.*

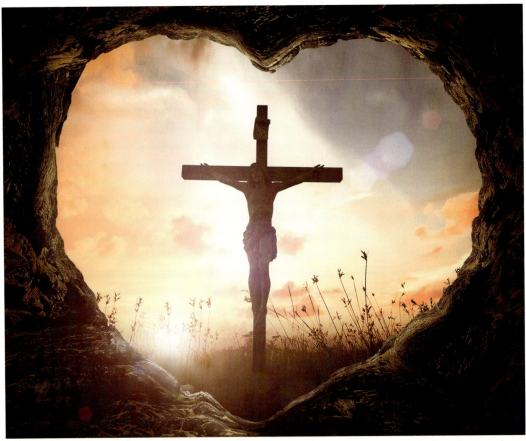

© Jacob_09/shutterstock.com

Commit—Day 3
Lectio: God's Law of Love

The longest psalm in the Bible is also a brilliantly constructed acrostic poem that celebrates the law (*Torah*) of the Lord as a rule of life that shines with beauty, life, power to save, and an unparalleled capacity to bring joy. Each of the twenty-two, eight-line stanzas of Psalm 119 starts with a different letter of the Hebrew alphabet, and the same letter begins every line in each stanza. In addition, every octet is built on numerous different words for "law" that add depth and richness. The psalm is both a monument to clever wordsmithing and a tribute to the creative power of the divine Word that finds expression in the law. As Pope Benedict said, "This Psalm is steeped in love for the word of God whose beauty, saving power and capacity for giving joy and life it celebrates; because the divine Law is not the heavy yoke of slavery but a liberating gift of grace that brings happiness . . . . 'Oh, how I love your law! It is my meditation all the day' (v. 97)" (General Audience, November 9, 2011).

This *lectio* exercise will reflect on just one stanza: Psalm 119:33–40.

> **Lectio:** The practice of praying with Scripture, *lectio divina* begins with an active and close reading of the Scripture passage. Read the verse below and then answer the questions to take a closer look at some of the details of the passage.

Teach me, O Lord, the way of your statutes; and I will keep it to the end.
Give me understanding, that I may keep your law
  and observe it with my whole heart.
Lead me in the path of your commandments, for I delight in it.
Incline my heart to your testimonies, and not to gain!
Turn my eyes from looking at vanities; and give me life in your ways.
Confirm to your servant your promise, which is for those who fear you.
Turn away the reproach which I dread; for your ordinances are good.
Behold, I long for your precepts; in your righteousness give me life!

—Psalm 119:33–40

SESSION 2

NOT JUST FIRE INSURANCE

After reading the passage several times, fill in the chart below. Each verse is spelled out in the first column for ease of reference. For each one, write down the way God's law is described; tell what the psalmist asks for, if anything; and write what he promises to do or the result he expects. The first one is filled in for you.

Verse	Description of Law	Thing Asked For	Promise / Result
33 "Teach me, O Lord, the way of your statutes; and I will keep it to the end."	(the way of your) Statutes	Teach them to me	I will keep its way to the end
34 "Give me understanding, that I may keep your law and observe it with my whole heart."			
35 "Lead me in the path of your commandments, for I delight in it."			
36 "Incline my heart to your testimonies, and not to gain!"			
37 "Turn my eyes from looking at vanities; and give me life in your ways."			
38 "Confirm to your servant your promise, which is for those who fear you."			
39 "Turn away the reproach which I dread; for your ordinances are good."			
40 "Behold, I long for your precepts; in your righteousness give me life!"			

When you are finished, go back and highlight the words or phrases that stand out to you, noting any similarities or contrasts.

> **MEDITATIO:** *Lectio*, a close reading and rereading of Scripture, is followed by *meditatio*, a time to reflect on the Scripture passage and to ponder the reason for particular events, descriptions, details, phrases, and even echoes from other Scripture passages that were noticed during *lectio*. Take some time now to meditate on the above verse.

SESSION 2

NOT JUST FIRE INSURANCE

The Law of the Lord, the object of the passionate love of the Psalmist as well as of every believer, is a source of life. The desire to understand it, to observe it and to direct the whole of one's being by it is the characteristic of every righteous person who is faithful to the Lord, and who "on his law . . . meditates day and night", as Psalm 1 recites (v. 2) . . . . The Law of God, at the centre of life, demands that the heart listen. It is a listening that does not consist of servile but rather of filial, trusting and aware obedience. Listening to the word is a personal encounter with the Lord of life, an encounter that must be expressed in concrete decisions and become a journey and a "sequela" [consequence]. When Jesus is asked what one should do to inherit eternal life he points to the way of observance of the Law but indicates what should be done to bring it to completion: "but you lack one thing; go, sell what you have, and give to the poor, and you will have treasure in heaven; and come, follow me!" (Mk 10:21ff.). Fulfilment of the Law is the following of Jesus, travelling on the road that Jesus took, in the company of Jesus.

—Pope Benedict XVI, General Audience, November 9, 2011

Re-read the words you circled in the chart on the previous page. What are they? Write them down here. Is there any connection between them? What stood out to you about those words?

_____
_____
_____

Read the Scripture again closely, hearing how the psalmist relates to God. What do these verses imply about who God is, about his desires, and how we may approach him?

_____
_____
_____

Read the passage one more time, then write your own verse to add to the end. Think of what God's Word/law/instruction has meant in your life. Praise him for it. Ponder like Mary. What words are most meaningful to you? Which give you life or joy? Choose a verse you like and use it as an example to address your own plea or praise to God.

_____
_____
_____

SESSION 2   NOT JUST FIRE INSURANCE

> **ORATIO, CONTEMPLATIO, RESOLUTIO:** Having read and meditated on today's Scripture passage, take some time to pray, to bring your thoughts to God (*oratio*), and to be receptive to God's grace in silence (*contemplatio*). Then end your prayer by making a simple concrete resolution (*resolutio*) to respond to God's prompting of your heart in today's prayer.

_____

_____

Let us therefore permit the Lord to instil this love for his word in our hearts and to grant that we may always place him and his holy will at the centre of our life. Let us ask that our prayers and the whole of our life be illuminated by the word of God, the lamp to light our footsteps and a light on our path, as Psalm 119 (cf. 105) says, so that we may walk safely in the land of men. And may Mary, who generously welcomed the Word, be our guide and comfort, the polestar that indicates the way to happiness.
—Pope Benedict XVI, General Audience, November 9, 2011

Commit—Day 4
Salvation as Knowing the Lord

God, infinitely perfect and blessed in himself, in a plan of sheer goodness freely created man to make him share in his own blessed life. For this reason, at every time and in every place, God draws close to man. He calls man to seek him, to know him, to love him with all his strength. He calls together all men, scattered and divided by sin, into the unity of his family, the Church. To accomplish this, when the fullness of time had come, God sent his Son as Redeemer and Savior. In his Son and through him, he invites men to become, in the Holy Spirit, his adopted children and thus heirs of his blessed life.
—Catechism of the Catholic Church, 1

Father, . . . this is eternal life, that they may know you, the only true God, and Jesus Christ whom you have sent.
—John 17:1–3

"This is eternal life," not "to escape punishment and Hell," but to know God the Father and his Son Jesus Christ. Imagine! God, Creator and Ruler of the universe, not only invites us to share in his life, but he also created us for that life! That's the whole reason for the law, as we learned earlier. "The law" (*Torah*) is both a love story between God and his people and also fatherly wisdom showing us what we're made for and how we can find fulfillment in him. It's like how somebody once used an acronym to describe the Bible:

"Basic Instructions Before Leaving Earth"

What we learn in God's Word, when we follow it, doesn't just give us a "get-out-of-Hell-free" card. It prepares us for Heaven.

SESSION 2

At the top of the previous page is the very first thing you read when you open the *Catechism*. It is a summary of why we are here. Read it carefully as something written to you, yourself. What strikes you?

_____

_____

_____

Salvation is not just a matter of us trying to escape something we see coming. It is God reaching out to us in love, inviting us to enter into the communion of love that already exists in him. As St. John, the beloved disciple, reminds us, "God *is* love" (1 John 4:8, emphasis added). Love is the very essence of who he is because the one true God is a communion of three divine persons. God is love because the Father loves the Son and the Son loves the Father and the love they share is the Holy Spirit.

You are on this earth because God wanted you to share that love and live in it forever. He doesn't just say, "Go on your own way and imitate me; love me and other people." Rather, he invites us to live in him while he lives in us, to immerse us in the life of love that he is and fill us with that life so that, as we receive it, this life of love can overflow to others.

God put us in the world to know, to love, and to serve him, and so to come to paradise. Beatitude makes us "partakers of the divine nature" and of eternal life. With beatitude, man enters into the glory of Christ and into the joy of the Trinitarian life.
—*Catechism of the Catholic Church*, 1721

As anyone who has truly loved and been loved is aware, a loving emotion is not enough. True love involves personal knowledge and relationship. It involves commitment. It involves mutual self-giving. All of this is found in the love that is God and the love God shows us and the love God invites us to live in and share. It's a beautiful cycle: God's love for us prompts us to love him; we receive his love and it overflows to others; we come to know him as we meditate on his love and, even more so, as we in turn love others. As it says in 1 John 4:7–8, 12, "Beloved, let us love one another; for love is of God, and he who loves is born of God and knows God. He who does not love does not know God; for God is love. . . . [I]f we love one another, God abides in us and his love is perfected in us."

This is what we were made for. In this is joy and abundant life!

In closing, meditate on Ephesians 3:14–21. Thank the Lord for his love, for his work in your life. What is one way you can come to know God better and be more "rooted and grounded in love" this week?

_____

_____

_____

The Adoration of the Trinity, Albrecht Dürer
© wikiart.org

Commit—Day 5
Truth and Beauty

Moses Breaks the Tables of the Law
by Paul Gustave Doré

Moses Breaks the Tables of the Law, Gustave Doré
© commons.wikimedia.org

Paul Gustave Doré was a prolific French illustrator whose talents included wood engraving, printmaking, painting, and sculpting. Doré was commissioned to produce illustrations for numerous literary works including Dante's *The Divine Comedy*, Cervantes's *Don Quixote*, and Milton's *Paradise Lost*, among others. In the mid 1860s, Doré was asked to design illustrations for a new deluxe edition of the French translation of the Vulgate Bible. Doré designed 241 wood engravings that were used to produce illustrations for the project that was published in 1866.

Doré provided two illustrations for chapter 32 of the Book of Exodus. The first image is that of Moses as he "went down from the mountain with the two tables [or tablets] of the covenant in his hands, tables that were written on both sides; on the one side and on the other were they written. And the tables were the work of God" (Exodus 32:15–16). The second illustration, which is the artwork for today's reflection, is that of Moses as he breaks the tablets of the law.

Moses's descending Mount Sinai with the tablets of the law is the climax of the entire Exodus story. From the opening chapters of the Book of Exodus, which found the people of Israel in slavery, through Moses's miraculous rescue from the Pharaoh's demonic order that all male Hebrew infants be drowned in the Nile River, continuing with the repeated plagues and Israel's wondrous passage through the Red Sea and the destruction of Pharaoh's chariots and charioteers, all these astonishing events propel the narrative to its climax where God himself descends upon Mount Sinai and Israel enters into a covenant with the God of their fathers.

The sight of Moses descending the mountain with the tablets written by God's own hand was to be a moment of national rejoicing, a celebration of thanksgiving for God's salvific work and the covenant into which Israel had entered. But rather than a celebration of the new covenant relationship, as he descends the mountain Moses sees something he could not have imagined: the people, who only a few chapters earlier had entered into a covenant with the God of Heaven and earth, have apostatized and are now worshipping a golden idol. The expected glorious climax of the Exodus story swiftly turns to tragedy.

In the illustrated Bible, the following scriptural verse was included underneath the image: "And as soon as he came near the camp and saw the calf and the dancing, Moses' anger burned hot, and he threw the tables out of his hands and broke them" (Exodus 32:19). Doré captures this moment, with Moses and the tablets of the Ten Commandments taking center stage. Moses's robes blow with the wind as he raises the stone tablets high in the air. The power of the moment is highlighted by the bolt of lightning streaking through the sky. The stone tablets, with the words of God etched on them, are highlighted by the bright light in the heavens, the origin of the lightning. With the verse from Exodus 32:19 below the picture, the viewer anticipates that at any second the stone tablets are to be shattered as they hit the steps at the base of the picture.

As Moses approaches "near the camp," Doré portrays several individuals below Moses in the image, each in different postures. One raises his hands, hailing Moses's arrival, and several look up in astonishment that after his delay up on the mountain Moses has actually returned. The first words written on the tablets forbade Israel from having other gods before the Lord (see Exodus 20:2–3), and it is this very command that God's people have trespassed. Three men in the foreground appear to display remorse for so great a sin—one clasps at Moses's feet, one with dread spread across his face raises his clasped hands to Heaven, and one slumps back unable to even look at Moses and the tablets he holds.

Doré's numerous and powerful images in the 1866 illustrated Bible brought to life key moments of the story of salvation, engaging readers to enter more deeply into the text and encounter the author of history. By choosing to illustrate the moment before the tablets are actually broken, Doré seems to stop time, allowing the viewer to contemplate in his or her own life the times we have transgressed God's commands. The pause in the action almost begs the viewer to not waste another moment and repent of any sins so as not to suffer the consequences of a broken relationship with the Lord who loves each of us.

SESSION 2

Take a moment to journal your ideas, questions, or insights about this session. Write down thoughts you had that may not have been mentioned in the text or the discussion questions. List any personal applications you got from the lessons. What challenged you the most in the teachings? How might you turn what you've learned into specific action?

SESSION 3

Not without Cost

OPENING PRAYER

O God, who willed that your Only Begotten Son
should undergo the Cross to save the human race,
grant, we pray,
that we, who have known his mystery on earth,
may merit the grace of his redemption in heaven,
through our Lord Jesus Christ, your Son,
who lives and reigns with you in the unity of the Holy Spirit,
one God, for ever and ever.
Amen.
—Collect, Feast of the Exaltation of the Holy Cross

INTRODUCTION

In the last session, we saw that salvation means more than just avoiding Hell and is, in fact, about having abundant life and knowing God's love. This raises the question: why the Cross? What do life and love have to do with suffering and death? To find the answer we must explore what Scripture says about sin as a debt and salvation as the ransom paid for us. When we do so, we discover that Christ's death on the Cross was not just a redeeming action but also a revelation of divine love.

© Doucefleur/shutterstock.com

Connect

How often do you make the Sign of the Cross? What does this prayer mean to you?

Do you think the crucifix is an uncomfortable image for many people? Why or why not?

© Watchara Ritjan/shutterstock.com

 ## Video

Watch the video segment. Use the outline below to follow along and take notes.

I. Why the Cross?
   A. Scripture uses economic language to discuss sin and redemption
      1. "Redemption" in modern usage—setting the wrong right
      2. "Redemption" in the ancient world—paying the cost of deliverance
   B. Debt
      1. Mosaic law provided for selling one's land or selling oneself into slavery to pay off debt
      2. Scripture talks about sin as a debt
      3. "[E]very one who commits sin is a slave of sin" (John 8:34)

SESSION 3

NOT WITHOUT COST

    C. Jesus, the Messiah, saves us from our sins (Matthew 1:21)
        1. The Son of man came "to give his life as a ransom *[lytron]* for many" (Matthew 20:28)
        2. Jesus's Death cancels our debt of sin (Colossians 2:13–14)

II. Why the price?
    A. Goal of salvation is entering into God's life of love (1 John 4:8–12)
    B. On the Cross, Christ shows us what it costs to be saved
        1. Sign of the Cross is a summary of the whole Gospel
        2. Cross reveals what it means to love like God
        3. What does it take to save our lives? (Mark 8:35)
    C. Israelites celebrated redemption from Egypt every Passover
        1. Part of celebration was almsgiving (John 13:27–30)
        2. Love your neighbor to show gratitude and love for God
        3. 2 Corinthians 8:1–15 and the inner logic of almsgiving
        4. We learn love in loving one another

DISCUSS

1. What was one thing from the video that you heard for the first time or that was an "aha" moment for you?

SESSION 3 — NOT WITHOUT COST

2. Why is the image of the crucifix so important? What purpose does this image serve that is not fulfilled by just an empty cross or even an image of the resurrected Lord?

   _____
   _____
   _____

3. There is a common saying that "salvation is free, but it isn't cheap." How does this saying fit with the discussion of Christ ransoming us from our debt of sin? What would you say is the "cost" of salvation?

   _____
   _____
   _____

4. What can you do to express your gratitude to God for paying the price of your redemption?

   _____
   _____
   _____

Quotes, Tips, & Definitions

Christ, the final Adam, by the revelation of the mystery of the Father and His love, fully reveals man to man himself and makes his supreme calling clear.

—*Gaudium et Spes*, 22

SESSION 3   NOT WITHOUT COST

MEMORY VERSE

In this the love of God was made manifest among us, that God sent his only-begotten Son into the world, so that we might live through him.

—1 John 4:9

CLOSING PRAYER

O most Holy Trinity,
I adore you
who dwell by your grace in my soul.
Sanctify me more and more,
make me love you more and more,
abide with me evermore
and be my true joy.
Amen.

FOR FURTHER READING

Brant Pitre, Michael P. Barber and John A. Kincaid, *Paul* (Grand Rapids: Eerdmans, 2019)

Catechism of the Catholic Church, 599–605 ("Christ's Redemptive Death in God's Plan of Salvation") and 606–618 ("Christ Offered Himself to His Father for Our Sins")

Gary Anderson, *Sin: A History* (Yale, 2009)

Commit—Day 1
Redemption and the Debt of Sin

Debt seems to be something we simultaneously abhor and accept as a fact of life. There are many things that are generally assumed to require going into debt in our modern society: a university degree, a new car, a house. Yet no one really wants to be in debt, and there are a multitude of resources out there for avoiding or getting out of debt.

© TierneyMJ/shutterstock.com

Have you ever been in debt? If so, what circumstances led to being in debt? How did you feel about it? If not, how would you feel about being in debt?

_____
_____
_____

So much of our economic activity revolves around avoiding or getting out of debt. The consequences for failing to pay back financial debt are too serious to ignore—a ruined credit score, bankruptcy, or even prison. But the consequences for failing to address our debt of sin are infinitely greater: eternal separation from God, who created us and loves us.

The economic terms the Bible uses to talk about sin and redemption paint a vivid picture of God's gift of salvation. God established his covenant with his people, creating a familial bond of love. God is ever faithful; he always upholds his end of the covenant (as we find throughout Scripture; see Deuteronomy 7:9 and 2 Timothy 2:13 for two examples). We, however, fail to live up to the terms of the covenant (see Romans 3:23). Ultimately sin is nothing other than a failure to love God as we ought to love him. Scripture describes this failure as a debt: in our covenant relationship we owe God our love, but we have failed to give him the love that we owe and have fallen into debt.

On our own we are completely incapable of paying our debt, and so we need a redeemer to pay the ransom and free us. The Mosaic law provided for just such a situation.

Look up Leviticus 25:47–49. Who was called to redeem a person from slavery resulting from debt? What light does this shed on God's role as described in Isaiah 54:5–8 and 63:16?

_____
_____
_____

Scripture refers to the Lord over and over as Israel's *goel*, the Hebrew word for "redeemer." Just as a person who sold himself into slavery to pay off his debt could be redeemed by his kinsman (his *goel*), Israel looked to God to rescue them from their oppressors. This redemption was both physical and spiritual (as we see in the Exodus, where God redeemed Israel from both physical slavery to Pharaoh and spiritual slavery to the false gods of Egypt).

Israel can not only ask for but also expectantly look to God to redeem them because of the covenant. A covenant forms family bonds. The above verses from Isaiah emphasize not only God's role as redeemer, but also his intimate love for Israel—which is even stronger than the love of a husband for his bride, or a father for his children.

Psalm 44:26 calls on this love God has for his people: "Rise up, come to our help! Deliver us for the sake of your merciful love!" Do you have confidence in God's readiness to come to your aid as your redeemer? If so, what gives you this confidence? If not, why not?

_____
_____
_____

But now thus says the LORD,
he who created you, O Jacob,
he who formed you, O Israel:
"Fear not, for I have redeemed you;
I have called you by name, you are mine."
—Isaiah 43:1

© Art Stocker/shutterstock.com

Commit—Day 2
Redemption and Atonement

You are probably familiar with the term "good news" as applied to the Gospel's message. In fact, the Greek word we translate as "gospel," *euangelion*, literally means "good message." But in order to fully appreciate the good news of God's salvation, we have to understand how serious the bad news of our sin really is. We have explored the idea of sin as a debt resulting in our slavery and from which Christ redeems us. This redemption takes place in the context of covenant—Jesus is our *goel*, the kinsman-redeemer come to our rescue. But he rescues us not merely from debt—nor even the imprisonment or slavery that could arise from debt—but from death. As our redeemer he makes atonement for our debt of sin, saving us from the spiritual death that results from sin.

To atone literally means to set "at one." Atonement, then, is the action that reconciles two parties. In the context of the covenant, atonement becomes necessary when Israel breaks the covenant with God a mere forty days after having entered into it (see Exodus). Moses seeks to make atonement for Israel's sin so that God will spare the people from the covenant curse of death they have incurred (see Exodus 32:30). God then makes provisions in his law for sacrifices for individual sin offerings as well as for the annual celebration of Yom Kippur, the Day of Atonement.

The Day of Atonement is one of the major holy days of the Jewish liturgical year. God lays out the law for the celebration of this day in Leviticus 16. On the tenth day of the seventh month (September/October in the Gregorian calendar) the Israelites were to observe a solemn fast and do no work. The sacrifices for the Day of Atonement included a bull as a sin offering for the high priest and two goats as a sin offering for the people. One goat was sacrificed. The other goat was sent away into the wilderness to "bear all [Israel's] iniquities upon him to a solitary land" (Leviticus 16:22). The high priest brought the blood of the sin offerings into the Holy of Holies to offer it to God.

The sacrifices for atonement reconciled Israel to God by serving as a kind of annual ransom—a payment that delivers the people from the consequence of their sin. These ransoms, imperfect and incomplete, were merely a precursor to the final and perfect atonement for sin. They point forward to the once-for-all atoning sacrifice of Christ.

SESSION 3

NOT WITHOUT COST

> **MEDITATIO:** *Lectio*, a close reading and rereading of Scripture, is followed by *meditatio*, a time to reflect on the Scripture passage and to ponder the reason for particular events, descriptions, details, phrases, and even echoes from other Scripture passages that were noticed during *lectio*. Take some time now to meditate on the above verse.

Through the Cross of Christ man is redeemed and Adam's experience is reversed. Adam, created in the image and likeness of God, claimed to be like God through his own effort, to put himself in God's place and in this way lost the original dignity that had been given to him. Jesus, instead, was "in the form of God" but humbled himself, immersed himself in the human condition, in total faithfulness to the Father, in order to redeem the Adam who is in us and restore to man the dignity he had lost. The Fathers emphasize that he made himself obedient, restoring to human nature, through his own humanity and obedience, what had been lost through Adam's disobedience. . . .

The Incarnation and the Cross remind us that complete fulfilment lies in conforming our human will to the will of the Father, in emptying ourselves of our selfishness, to fill ourselves with God's love, with his charity, and thereby become capable of truly loving others.

Man does not find himself by remaining closed in on himself, by affirming himself. Man finds himself only by coming out of himself; only if we come out of ourselves do we find ourselves. And if Adam wanted to imitate God, this was not a bad thing in itself but he had the wrong idea of God. God is not someone who only wants greatness. God is love which was already given in the Trinity and was then given in the Creation. And imitating God means coming out of oneself, giving oneself in love.

—Pope Benedict XVI, General Audience, June 27, 2012

The meditation contrasts Adam, who tried to make himself like God by his own effort, with Christ, who did not "count equality with God a thing to be grasped." What temptations do you use to grasp at equality with God? What can you do to resist these temptations?

_____
_____

What does it mean to truly imitate God? What do you think this looks like in your life?

_____
_____

Jesus was "obedient unto death, even death on a cross." What radical act of obedience does God want from you? What do you stand to lose by that obedience? What do you stand to gain?

_____
_____

SESSION 3

NOT WITHOUT COST

> **ORATIO, CONTEMPLATIO, RESOLUTIO:** Having read and meditated on today's Scripture passage, take some time to pray, to bring your thoughts to God (*oratio*), and to be receptive to God's grace in silence (*contemplatio*). Then end your prayer by making a simple concrete resolution (*resolutio*) to respond to God's prompting of your heart in today's prayer.

_____

_____

He became man who was God, by receiving what He was not, not by losing what He was: so God became man. There you have something for your weakness, something for your perfection. Let Christ raise you by that which is man, lead you by that which is God-man, and guide you through to that which is God.

—St. Augustine (*Tractate on the Gospel of John*, 23, 6)

© Zwiebackesser/shutterstock.com

COMMIT—DAY 4
THE CROSS AS THE REVELATION OF DIVINE LOVE

"God is love" (1 John 4:8). How do we know? We know because "the Bible tells me so," as the children's song says, but also because God reveals this truth not only in his Word but in his mighty deeds. How has God revealed his love in your life?

_____
_____
_____

Provision in times of need, abundant blessings, answered prayers, creation itself—God reveals his love to us in a wide variety of ways. But the fullest revelation of his love comes when he pours himself out for us on the Cross.

[A]nd I, when I am lifted up from the earth, will draw all men to myself.
—John 12:32 (Communion Antiphon, Feast of the Exaltation of the Holy Cross)

As we discovered in reflection on the great Christological hymn in Philippians 2:5–11, this outpouring of self in love is central to the divine life of the Trinity. It is also the way in which we become fully human in the image and likeness of God. As God, the Son empties himself to become man. As man, he empties himself in the humiliation of death on a cross. Thus, the Cross reveals both the innermost secret of the Trinity and God's incredible plan to make us partakers of his divine nature.

© mountainpix/shutterstock.com

Forgiveness of our sins is not the end of the story of salvation. Jesus pays our debt of sin and ransoms us from death so that we will be free to enter into communion with him now and for all eternity. The Cross shows us not only the extraordinary price that was paid for us but also the unfathomable love for which we were created.

SESSION 3

NOT WITHOUT COST

The personal relation of the Son to the Father is something that man cannot conceive of nor the angelic powers even dimly see: and yet, the Spirit of the Son grants a participation in that very relation to us who believe that Jesus is the Christ and that we are born of God.
—*Catechism of the Catholic Church*, 2780

God created us for love, and anything less than his love will leave us empty. When Jesus says that the commandments to love God and to love one's neighbor summarize all the law and the prophets (see Matthew 22:37–40), he is not just listing the rules that we need to obey to get to Heaven. He is laying out for us a road map to our ultimate fulfillment and happiness. How do we fulfill the commands to love God and neighbor? We are called to pour out our lives in love as Christ did. As absurd as it might seem, the Cross is the road map to happiness.

What does the world say about the purpose of being human and how to find happiness? How does this compare to what the Cross reveals about humanity and happiness?

_____

_____

_____

You learn to speak by speaking, to study by studying, to run by running, to work by working; and just so you learn to love God and man by loving. All those who think to learn in any other way deceive themselves.

—St. Francis de Sales

© Zwiebackesser/shutterstock.com

Consider 1 John 4:8–12 and the above quote from St. Francis de Sales. What is one concrete way you can grow in your love for God and neighbor this week?

___

___

___

Compassion, William-Adolphe Bouguereau
© commons.wikimedia.org

Commit—Day 5
Truth and Beauty

The Crucifixion
Pietro Lorenzetti, c.1340, The Metropolitan Museum of Art, New York

The Crucifixion, Pietro Lorenzetti
© shutterstock

Pietro Lorenzetti was an Italian painter of the Sienese school, along with his brother Ambrogio. While in Assisi working on a series of frescoes for the north transept of the lower church of the Basilica of St. Francis, Pietro encountered the work of Giotto, whom the biographer Vassari described as introducing "the technique of drawing accurately from life." Giotto's naturalism was to influence Pietro's later works, including this scene of the Crucifixion with its emotional intensity and realistic figures.

SESSION 3

Not without Cost

Read Luke 23:39–49 and John 19:25–35. Who is in the crowd on Calvary?

_____

_____

Pietro Lorenzetti's *The Crucifixion*, which measures 16.5 inches by 12.5 inches, is thought to be one of a series of small panels (another panel presents Christ before Pilate) that was likely a portable, folding altarpiece. The brilliant gold leaf work, the bright vermillion reds, and the deep lapis blues catch and hold the viewer's eye. At once one is drawn into the numerous figures of the multitude that fill the foreground at the foot of the Cross.

On the right, two Roman centurions sit upon their stately horses. One soldier points to Jesus using the end of his mace, and the hexagonal halo identifies him as the convert whom St. Luke describes saying, "Now when the centurion saw what had taken place, he praised God, and said, 'Certainly this man was innocent!'" (Luke 23:47).

Moving into the crowd and to the left, several women support the Blessed Mother, who appears limp, overwhelmed with grief at the death of her Son. St. John, the beloved disciple, draws close to this small group to lend his support of Jesus's mother, who is now, at Jesus's request, his mother also.

Behind the crowd, pairs of mounted soldiers appear to be monitoring the perimeter of the spectacle to prevent a riot from breaking out. The pair of mounted soldiers just behind the women carry long pointed spears. One, with hands folded in prayer, looks with adoration toward Jesus, and his hexagonal halo identifies him as Longinus, whom Tradition identifies as the soldier who pierced Jesus's side with a lance. Other soldiers and bystanders fill in the crowd at the foot of the Cross. A man in yellow can be seen wielding a club, ready to swing with full force in order to break the legs of the unrepentant thief.

As the viewer's attention is drawn upward, the two criminals crucified with Jesus appear on his right and left. The bloody legs of the thief on Jesus's right have already been broken and his body hangs limp, his head bowed to the ground and eyes closed now that life has left his body. But the halo surrounding his head confirms Jesus's words to the repentant thief: "Truly, I say to you, today you will be with me in Paradise" (Luke 23:43).

In the center of the painting, Jesus's lifeless body, ashen gray in color, hangs on the Cross. Having breathed his last, his knees buckle and the full weight of his body now stretches his arms to their full length. Love brought Jesus to Calvary, and because of his love he submitted to the nails and endured the agony of the Cross, but having given himself completely, the nails alone now hold his lifeless body to the Cross. Blood pours out of his chest at the point where the soldier's spear had pierced his side. Blood also falls from the wounds in his hands and feet, a reminder of the excruciating pain Jesus endured for our salvation. While later Renaissance painters will fill the background of Crucifixion scenes with detailed landscapes, Pietro Lorenzetti's painting retains the gold background of the pre-Renaissance, an effect that communicates the divine gift that is given on the Cross.

SESSION 3

Take a moment to journal your ideas, questions, or insights about this session. Write down thoughts you had that may not have been mentioned in the text or the discussion questions. List any personal applications you got from the lessons. What challenged you the most in the teachings? How might you turn what you've learned into specific action?

SESSION 4

NOT JUST PERSONAL

OPENING PRAYER

O God, who from living and chosen stones
prepare an eternal dwelling for your majesty,
increase in your Church the grace you have bestowed,
so that by unceasing growth
your faithful people may build up the heavenly Jerusalem.
Through our Lord Jesus Christ, your Son,
who lives and reigns with you in the unity of the Holy Spirit,
one God, for ever and ever.
Amen.
—Collect, On the Anniversary of the Dedication of a Church

INTRODUCTION

Salvation is not without cost, as we saw in the last session. We were not only "bought with a price" (1 Corinthians 6:20), but we were ransomed for a purpose—communion with the Most Holy Trinity. But that communion is not merely a personal relationship between us and Jesus. Our relationship with Jesus necessarily includes a relationship with his Body, the Church. In this session, we will explore the relationship between Christ and his Church and what it means for us and our salvation.

© Yuriy Golub/shutterstock.com

Connect

The poet John Donne famously remarked, "No man is an island." In what ways do you depend on other people? Who is dependent on you?

How would you respond if someone asked you what they needed to do to be saved?

Many people say they are "spiritual" but not "religious." What role do you think the Church plays in salvation?

© ZoneCreative/shutterstock

Video

Watch the video segment. Use the outline below to follow along and take notes.

I. Salvation is more than a personal relationship with Christ
   A. Necessity of a "vital and personal relationship" with God (*CCC*, 2558)
      1. Salvation is also a relationship with the Father and the Spirit
      2. Salvation is also a relationship with all those who are also "in Christ" (1 Corinthians 1:9)
   B. Baptism
      1. 1 Peter 3:21; Acts 2:38–40
      2. You can't baptize yourself—salvation takes place through Christ working through other people
      3. Not simply baptized into Christ but into the Body of Christ, the Church (1 Corinthians 12:12–13)
      4. Infant Baptism highlights the real dimension of grace in salvation
   C. The communion in which Christ wants us to share is effected by the Eucharist (1 Corinthians 10:16–17)

SESSION 4

NOT JUST PERSONAL

    D. Communal dimension of salvation is essential because God is a communion of Persons
II. No salvation outside the Church
    A. Doesn't mean that non-Catholics necessarily go to Hell
        1. Old Testament figures such as Abraham saved without Baptism (John 8:56)
        2. Good thief (Dismas) saved without Baptism (Luke 23:39–43)
    B. All saved by Christ through his Church
III. Images of the Church
    A. Body of Christ, Bride of Christ
    B. Church's holiness is dependent on Christ, not individual members

Discuss

1. What was one thing from the teaching that you heard for the first time or that was particularly enlightening or striking?

2. Salvation is about more than a personal relationship with Jesus—it also means a personal relationship with the Father and the Spirit, as well as a real union with everyone united to Christ in Baptism. Which of these relationships is easiest for you? Which is the hardest?

SESSION 4

3. If "no salvation outside of the Church" doesn't mean that non-Catholics or even non-Christians automatically go to Hell, is it still important for us to evangelize? Why or why not?

_____
_____
_____

4. As Dr. Barber says in the teaching, Christ gave everything for the Church. What do you do to show your love for the Church?

_____
_____
_____
_____

Quotes, Tips, & Definitions

About Jesus Christ and the Church, I simply know they're just one thing, and we shouldn't complicate the matter.

—St. Joan of Arc

MEMORY VERSE

For just as the body is one and has many members, and all the members of the body, though many, are one body, so it is with Christ. For by one Spirit we were all baptized into one body . . .

—1 Corinthians 12:12–13

SESSION 4

CLOSING PRAYER

O Blessed Joseph,
As once you rescued the Child Jesus from deadly peril,
so now protect God's Holy Church
from the snares of the enemy and from all adversity;
shield, too, each one of us by your constant protection,
so that, supported by your example and your aid,
we may be able to live piously, to die in holiness,
and to obtain eternal happiness in heaven.
Amen.
—Taken from the Prayer to St. Joseph after the Rosary by Pope Leo XIII

FOR FURTHER READING

Brant Pitre, "The Divine Love Story," *Jesus the Bridegroom: The Greatest Love Story Ever Told* (New York: Image, a division of Random House, 2014)

Catechism of the Catholic Church, 748–780 ("The Church in God's Plan"), 781–810 ("The Church—People of God, Body of Christ, Temple of the Holy Spirit"), 811–870 ("The Church Is One, Holy, Catholic, and Apostolic")

Commit—Day 1
The Church in the New Testament

At first glance, the Church seems to be an innovation of the New Covenant, since the word "church" is not found in the Old Testament—at least not in most English translations. But in fact, the word *ekklesia*, which is translated "church" in the New Testament, is used in the Septuagint (the Greek translation of the Old Testament) to refer to the assembly of God's people. In both the Old and New Testaments, the Church is God's chosen people.

© Rawpixel.com/shutterstock.com

CHURCH

The Greek word for "church," ekklesia, also means "assembly" or "congregation." It comes from the verb ekkalein, which means "to call out of." The English word "church" comes from the related Greek word kyriake, which means "belonging to the Lord."

Scripture speaks of the Church as the people called by God. What does it mean to be called by God individually? What does it mean to be called by God as part of a larger group?

_____

_____

_____

The New Testament authors give us further insight into what it means to be the covenant people of God. Specifically, the New Testament speaks of the Church as the Body of Christ, the new Temple of God, the Family of God, and the Bride of Christ.

St. Paul illustrates the real union believers have with one another in Christ by describing the Church as a Body of which Jesus is the Head (see Romans 12:4–5; 1 Corinthians 12:12–27; Ephesians 1:22–23; and Colossians 1:18). The Body of Christ carries on the mission of her Head, continuing the work of salvation that Jesus accomplished in his life, Death, and Resurrection. Our Lord was given the title Emmanuel, "God with us," and one way he remains present with us is in and through his Body, the Church.

Throughout his public ministry, Jesus reveals that he is the new Temple, the new dwelling place of God with his people (see, for example, John 2:19–21). Jesus refers to himself as the "cornerstone" (Mark 12:10), indicating that we also have a place to fill in this new Temple. Paul tells us clearly in 2 Corinthians 6:16 that "we are the temple of the living God," and Peter draws out the connection between Christ the cornerstone and the Church as Temple in 1 Peter 2:4–7. And in addition to calling the Church the Temple of God, Paul tells us that we are the "household of faith" (Galatians 6:10).

Finally, the New Testament calls the Church the Bride of Christ. In the Old Testament, God describes his relationship with Israel as that of a bridegroom and his bride (see Isaiah 54:5). John the Baptist refers to himself as "the friend of the bridegroom" (John 3:29), and Jesus refers to himself as the bridegroom (see Mark 2:18–20). Paul teaches on this great mystery of Christ and his Church in Ephesians 5:21–33.

The union of Christ with his Church is a great and glorious mystery. Family, Temple, Bride, and Body all describe the mystery of the union of Christ with his Church in related but slightly different ways. Read Ephesians 2:11–22 and 5:25–32. Which of these images speaks most profoundly to you at this point in your journey? Why?

_____

_____

_____

© sirtravelalot/shutterstock.com

THE MYSTERY OF THE HOLINESS OF THE CHURCH

How can we say the Church is holy when we see so much evidence to the contrary? Although the egregious crimes of some Church leaders and members throughout history cause particular scandal, we don't have to look any further than ourselves to find evidence of sin in the Holy Catholic Church. But we do not make the Church holy (or unholy); the Church, if we let her, makes us holy. Thus the Catechism *tells us that the Church is "unfailingly holy" because Christ has united her to himself, although her members are not yet perfectly holy (see* CCC, *823–829). As St. Paul VI wrote, "[The Church] is therefore holy, though she has sinners in her bosom, because she herself has no other life but that of grace: it is by living by her life that her members are sanctified; it is by removing themselves from her life that they fall into sins and disorders that prevent the radiation of her sanctity. This is why she suffers and does penance for these offenses, of which she has the power to heal her children through the blood of Christ and the gift of the Holy Spirit" (*Credo of the People of God, *19).*

Commit—Day 2
One Bread, One Body

If the Church is the Body of Christ in which we are all "individually members one of another," as St. Paul says in Romans 12:5, how do we become members of that Body? As Dr. Barber said in his teaching, "Salvation is sacramental." The sacraments—specifically the sacraments of initiation: Baptism, Confirmation, and the Holy Eucharist—are the means by which we become members of the Body of Christ and receive the salvation Christ has entrusted to his Church. We are born into the Body of Christ in Baptism, strengthened in Confirmation, and nourished in the Eucharist.

The *Catechism* describes Baptism as the "basis of the whole Christian life" and "the gateway to life in the Spirit" (*CCC*, 1213). Baptism makes us a part of the Body of Christ because in this sacrament we are baptized "into Christ Jesus," as Paul tells us in Romans 6:3–4, to share in his Death so that we may also rise with him to new life. If each person who is baptized is baptized into Christ, then Baptism also connects us to one another as members of one Body. "Baptism incorporates us *into the Church*" (*CCC*, 1267, emphasis in the original).

© Ruslan Lytvyn/shutterstock.com

The new life we receive in Baptism is then strengthened in Confirmation. This sacrament not only increases the gifts of the Holy Spirit in us and unites us more closely to Christ, but it also binds us more closely to the Church (see *CCC*, 1303).

Both Baptism and Confirmation (as well as all the other sacraments) are oriented toward the Eucharist, our "source and summit" (*CCC*, 1324). Read 1 Corinthians 10:16–17. How does Paul explain the relationship between the Eucharist and the Church as the Body of Christ?

_____

_____

_____

The *Catechism* tells us that the Eucharist is the source of both our communion with God and our union with one another in the Body of Christ (*CCC*, 1325). In other words, "the Eucharist makes the Church" (*CCC*, 1396).

The sacraments of healing (Penance and Anointing of the Sick) and the sacraments of service (Holy Orders and Holy Matrimony) also tell us that salvation is not just personal. Each sacrament bestows personal graces on the one receiving it, but the sacraments also bear fruit for the Church as a whole. The Sacrament of Penance reconciles us not only to God but also to his Church. In fact, we cannot be reconciled to one without being reconciled to another. And when we are healed from the wounds of our sin in this sacrament, the whole Church is revitalized (see *CCC*, 1469).

In a similar way, the Sacrament of Anointing of the Sick strengthens both the person receiving it and the Church. Through the grace of this sacrament, the sick person offers his or her suffering to God to contribute "to the sanctification of the Church and to the good of all men for whom the Church suffers" (*CCC*, 1522). Holy Orders and Holy Matrimony show even more plainly how our salvation is bound up with one another. The *Catechism* says that these sacraments of service are "directed toward the salvation of others; if they contribute as well to personal salvation, it is through service to others that they do so. They confer a particular mission in the Church and serve to build up the People of God" (*CCC*, 1534).

Salvation is sacramental. In what ways have the sacraments been formative in your own faith? Take some time to thank God for the gift of his sacraments, especially Baptism and the Eucharist.

_____

_____

> *Communion renews, strengthens, and deepens this incorporation into the Church, already achieved by Baptism. In Baptism we have been called to form but one body. The Eucharist fulfills this call.*
>
> —*Catechism of the Catholic Church*, 1396

© wideonet/shutterstock.com

Commit—Day 3
Lectio: Jesus Our Cornerstone

Jesus Christ invites us into a profound and intimate union with himself and his Church. As we draw closer to Christ, we also draw closer to everyone who is united to him through Baptism and the other sacraments. We have a place prepared for us, not separately and in isolation but rather incorporated into the temple of which he is the precious cornerstone.

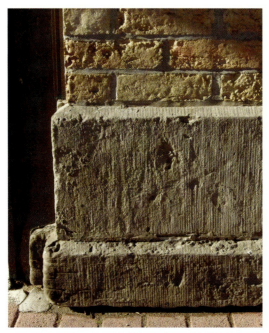

© Kerry Garvey/shutterstock.com

> **Lectio:** The practice of praying with Scripture, *lectio divina* begins with an active and close reading of the Scripture passage. Read the verse below and then answer the questions to take a closer look at some of the details of the passage.

Come to him, to that living stone, rejected by men but in God's sight chosen and precious; and like living stones be yourselves built into a spiritual house, to be a holy priesthood, to offer spiritual sacrifices acceptable to God through Jesus Christ. For it stands in Scripture:
> *"Behold, I am laying in Zion a stone, a cornerstone chosen and precious,*
> *and he who believes in him will not be put to shame."*

To you therefore who believe, he is precious, but for those who do not believe,
> *"The very stone which the builders rejected has become the cornerstone."*

—1 Peter 2:4–7

SESSION 4 NOT JUST PERSONAL

How many times does Peter use the word "stone"? How many kinds of stones does he talk about?
_____
_____
_____

How does Peter describe the stone(s)? What are they used for?
_____
_____
_____

What determines whether we value or reject the cornerstone?
_____
_____
_____

> **MEDITATIO:** *Lectio*, a close reading and rereading of Scripture, is followed by *meditatio*, a time to reflect on the Scripture passage and to ponder the reason for particular events, descriptions, details, phrases, and even echoes from other Scripture passages that were noticed during *lectio*. Take some time now to meditate on the above verse.

[T]he stone temple is the symbol of the living Church, the Christian community, that the Apostles Peter and Paul had, in their Letters, already understood as a "spiritual building", constructed by God with the "living stones" that are the Christians, upon the one foundation that is Jesus Christ, who is in turn compared to the "cornerstone" cf. 1 Cor 3: 9-11, 16-17; 1 Pt 2: 4-8; Eph 2: 20-22). "Brethren, ... you are God's building", St Paul writes, and he adds, "God's temple is holy, and you are that temple" (1 Cor 3: 9c, 17). The beauty and the harmony of churches, destined to render praise to God, invites us human beings too, though limited and sinful, to convert ourselves to form a "cosmos", a well-ordered construction, in close communion with Jesus, who is the true Holy of Holies. This reaches its culmination in the Eucharistic liturgy, in which the "ecclesia" that is, the community of baptized finds itself again united to listen to the Word of God and nourish itself on the Body and Blood of Christ. Gathered around this twofold table, the Church of living stones builds herself up in truth and in love and is moulded interiorly by the Holy Spirit, transforming herself into what she receives, conforming herself ever more to her Lord Jesus Christ. She herself, if she lives in sincere and fraternal unity, thus becomes a spiritual sacrifice pleasing to God.
—Pope Benedict XVI, Angelus Address, November 9, 2008,
Feast of the Dedication of the Basilica of St. John Lateran

SESSION 4 — NOT JUST PERSONAL

What do you think it means for you to be a "living stone" built into a "spiritual house"?

_____
_____
_____

Peter talks about the living stones being a "holy priesthood" offering "spiritual sacrifices." What does this mean in reference to the Church as a whole? What does it mean for you?

_____
_____
_____

What does it mean that Jesus is the cornerstone of the Church? What does it mean that you are built onto this cornerstone?

_____
_____
_____

> **ORATIO, CONTEMPLATIO, RESOLUTIO:** Having read and meditated on today's Scripture passage, take some time to pray, to bring your thoughts to God (*oratio*), and to be receptive to God's grace in silence (*contemplatio*). Then end your prayer by making a simple concrete resolution (*resolutio*) to respond to God's prompting of your heart in today's prayer.

_____
_____
_____

It is only within the faith of the Church that each of the faithful can believe.
—Catechism of the Catholic Church, 1253

Commit—Day 4
Is There Salvation outside the Church?

We need other people. This fact is entirely self-evident in nearly all areas of life. We literally cannot exist without the help of other people because we receive life from our parents. And no matter how independent and self-sufficient we may become, we still rely on others in countless—and perhaps unappreciated—ways. We are social creatures, and the help of other people increases our happiness and our ability to thrive in this life.

What would your life look like without any community?

_____
_____
_____

God obviously created us for community here on earth; he also created us for eternal communion. As we have seen in previous sessions, this eternal communion is precisely what salvation is: knowing God's love and participating now and forever in the divine life of the Trinity.

Knowing how much we need other people in this life, it should come as no surprise that God's plan to save us involves the help of other people—specifically, the Church. This help is not just the support of a community of like-minded people all striving for the same goal, although that sort of help is very useful. The Church is necessary to our salvation because God has established his Church as "an instrument for the redemption of all" and "the universal sacrament of salvation" (*Lumen Gentium*, 9, 48).

© Rawpixel.com/shutterstock.com

SESSION 4

Just as we are not the source of our own physical life, we cannot give spiritual life to ourselves. As we saw in the earlier discussion of the sacraments, we receive new life in Baptism, strength in Confirmation, nourishment in the Eucharist, and healing in Penance and Anointing. All of these life-giving and life-sustaining gifts we receive from the Church at the hands of a bishop, priest, or deacon. We cannot provide any of them for ourselves. Thus, we need the Church in order to receive Christ's salvation through the sacraments: "All salvation comes from Christ the Head through the Church which is his Body" (*CCC*, 846).

These assertions may sound as if the Church is saying that all non-Catholics automatically go to Hell, but that is not what the Church teaches. As the *Catechism* makes clear in paragraph 1257, God has chosen to make Baptism the ordinary means of salvation, but he is free to work by extraordinary means.

Christ is the only way to the Father: "I am the way, and the truth, and the life; no one comes to the Father, but by me" (John 14:6). Because of the union of Christ and his Church, to say that there is salvation outside (or without) the Church would be like saying there is salvation without Jesus. That claim is obviously unbiblical. But Scripture does provide many examples of people who were saved although they had no explicit knowledge of Jesus.

Read Hebrews 11. Who are some of the examples of faith and righteousness cited in this passage? What relation did they have to Christ in life? What relation do they have to Christ and the Church now, according to Hebrews 12:1–2?

_____

_____

_____

The righteous men and women of the Old Testament could not have an explicit faith in Jesus because they lived and died before he came into the world. And yet, because of the faith they did have, they also are saved through Christ and are even held up as models of faith and described as cheering on those of us still running the race. From the faith they demonstrated during their lives we can deduce that they would have believed in Christ and desired Baptism had they had the chance.

The understanding that God can work outside of the Sacrament of Baptism to save people might seem to imply that evangelization is not an urgent issue. If non-Catholics and even non-Christians can still be saved, why bother trying to convert anyone? The *Catechism* answers that Baptism is the only sure means of salvation, and of course we have Christ's command to go out and baptize, which we are obliged to obey (*CCC*, 1257; Matthew 28:19–20). Knowing the incredible life that each person is called to in Christ, both in Heaven as well as here and now, propels us to ardently share the Gospel with everyone we meet.

SESSION 4

NOT JUST PERSONAL

How does understanding the role of the Church in God's plan of salvation affect your relationship with the Church?

_____
_____
_____

For there is no entering into salvation outside the Church, just as in the time of the deluge there was none outside the Ark, which denotes the Church.
—St. Thomas Aquinas (*Summa Theologica*, III.q73.a.3)

Paradise, Giovanni di Paolo
© Everett - Art/shutterstock.com

Commit—Day 5
Truth and Beauty

The Adoration of the Trinity
Albrecht Dürer, 1509–1511, Kunsthistorisches Museum, Vienna, Austria

The Adoration of the Trinity, Albrecht Dürer
© commons.wikimedia.org

Albrecht Dürer was a German painter and printmaker during the time of the Northern Renaissance (beginning in the late fifteenth century). While he was born and later set up his own workshop in Nuremberg, he traveled to other parts of Europe, including Italy, where he was in contact with, and influenced by, important Italian artists of his time. *Adoration of the Trinity* (also known as the Landauer Altarpiece) is one of Dürer's finest works and was commissioned by Matthäus Landauer. Landauer was a wealthy businessman who established the Twelve Brothers House, a charitable institution that housed up to twelve elderly craftsmen who were unable to support themselves. Landauer commissioned Dürer to produce an altarpiece for the institution's chapel, which was dedicated to the Holy Trinity and all the saints. The painting itself measures nearly 4.5 feet by 4 feet and was originally housed in an ornately carved frame, which itself included the Landauer coat of arms and a scene of the Last Judgment.

SESSION 4   NOT JUST PERSONAL

Look up the following verses. How is the court of Heaven described?

Revelation 19:6–7: _____

_____

_____

Revelation 20:11: _____

_____

_____

Revelation 21:1–3: _____

_____

_____

The central focus of the painting is the Holy Trinity. God the Father appears enthroned in the heavens, his head donning an intricately decorated crown while angels extend the folds of his rich, green robe. God the Father supports the Cross on which Jesus his Son is nailed, and angels around the throne present instruments of the Passion (stone pillar of the flagellation, spear with the sponge that was dipped in hyssop, etc.). Above Father and Son the dove of the Holy Spirit is seen, arrayed in golden light and encircled by countless cherubs. This image of the Trinity, with the Father presenting the Cross of Christ, is often referred to as the Throne of Grace.

Surrounding the heavenly throne are the saints, raised up to the heavenly Jerusalem to join with the angels in worship of God. The heavenly assembly is divided into four quadrants. Closest to the throne, on the viewer's right, are male saints, amongst whom are the Old Testament prophets and kings, including King David playing his harp and Moses holding the tablets of the Law. These are led by a kneeling St. John the Baptist, the last of the Old Testament prophets and herald of the Messiah Jesus Christ. The expected representatives of the Apostles, Evangelists, and Church Fathers are likely missing in the painting because they appeared in the original stained glass windows of the chapel. To the left of the throne, Mary the Mother of God leads a group of female saints and martyrs holding palm branches, amongst whom can be seen St. Agnes holding a lamb, St. Catherine holding a wheel and sword, and St. Barbara holding the chalice and Host.

Below these two groups are men and women of the Church. On the left are religious men and women of all levels from the pope and a cardinal to a simple monk in his hooded, brown robe. Amongst these religious, Dürer has included his laymen patron, Matthäus Landauer, holding his hat and to whom the cardinal extends his hand. On the right are secular men and women of all levels, from the emperor and those finely dressed to a peasant with uncovered head holding a threshing flail. On the earth below the heavenly scene, Dürer has included a self-portrait in the bottom right of the painting, where he stands pointing to a sign that reads, "Albrecht Dürer of the North made this in the year of the Virgin 1511."

The Adoration of the Trinity in its original frame

Given the Last Judgment scene on the frame, the painting appears to portray the heavenly entry of the members of Christ's Body, the Church, whose virtuous lives, by the grace and mercy of Christ's sacrifice on the Cross, now enter into the kingdom of Heaven and behold God face to face. The painting is thought by many to image the writing of the final book of St. Augustine's *City of God*, where Augustine reflects on "the eternal bliss of the City of God." Given its position over the chapel's altar, the painting also has Eucharistic significance. Given its location above the altar, the image of God's Throne of Mercy would have appeared just behind the elevated Host during the Eucharistic consecration, a reminder that the Mass being celebrated in the Twelve Brothers House chapel was a foretaste of the heavenly worship the congregation hoped to participate in for eternity. The congregation in the chapel, in a sense, joined the saints depicted in Dürer's painting in worship of God, who paid the price of our salvation by the Cross of Jesus Christ.

SESSION 4

Take a moment to journal your ideas, questions, or insights about this session. Write down thoughts you had that may not have been mentioned in the text or the discussion questions. List any personal applications you got from the lessons. What challenged you the most in the teachings? How might you turn what you've learned into specific action?

_____
_____
_____
_____
_____
_____
_____
_____
_____
_____
_____
_____
_____
_____
_____
_____
_____
_____
_____
_____
_____
_____
_____
_____
_____
_____
_____
_____
_____
_____
_____

SESSION 5

Not Just a Legal Transaction

OPENING PRAYER

Stir up your power, O Lord,
and come to our help with mighty strength,
that what our sins impede
the grace of your mercy may hasten.
Through our Lord Jesus Christ, your Son,
who lives and reigns with you in the unity of the Holy Spirit,
one God, for ever and ever. Amen.
—Collect, First Week of Advent

INTRODUCTION

After the Fall, each person is born not only with the stain of sin on their soul but also with a fallen human nature. Thanks be to God that his gift of salvation not only frees us from Original Sin but also transforms us from the inside out, healing the root of our brokenness: our hearts. As we will see in this session, salvation is not simply a legal transaction by which we are *declared* righteous, but by the gift of God's Spirit we are actually *made* righteous.

© Evgeny Atamanenko/shutterstock.com

CONNECT

Have you ever "gotten off the hook" for something that you knew you should have been punished for? What was that experience like?

Have you ever been in a situation where someone began to distance themselves from you because they did not feel you would forgive them for something they did? Were you able to forgive them? How did that affect the relationship?

VIDEO

Watch the video segment. Use the outline below to follow along and take notes.

I. Salvation—Not just a legal transaction
   A. Called to be conformed to the image of God's Son
      1. Salvation is a family matter
      2. Impossible without God's help
   B. Fallen humanity unable to do good (Romans 7:15–19)
      1. We need circumcision of the heart
      2. We need God to fix our hearts

II. The New Covenant (Jeremiah 31:31–34 and Ezekiel 36:26–27)
   A. Law within humanity (2 Corinthians 3:3–6)
   B. Transformation of the heart, by forgiveness of sin and gift of the Spirit

III. Justification
   A. No perfect translations
      1. To make righteous, to "rightify"
      2. Has legal dimension (Exodus 23; Deuteronomy 25; 1 Corinthians 4)
   B. Reformed Protestant approach on the meaning of "justification"
      1. By grace
      2. Justification is a change in legal status only—one who is guilty is declared not guilty
      3. Righteousness is external to the believer (Philippians 3:9)
      4. Transformation is a part of sanctification

SESSION 5 — Not Just a Legal Transaction

C. Catholic position
   1. By grace
   2. Justification is a legal decree, but not only a legal decree
   3. Justification is also transformative, because God effects what he declares
   4. Ministry of righteousness (Romans 5:17–21; 2 Corinthians 5:21)
D. Importance of having a proper understanding
   1. Salvation is not just a legal exchange
   2. Grace allows us to be remade in the likeness of Christ

Discuss

1. What new insights did you gain from Dr. Barber's teaching on the transformation of the heart and God's desire to transform us from within?

2. Why do people have such a strong tendency to keep sinning? What is God's plan to solve this? What role does the Spirit play in God's plan?

3. One of the effects of the New Covenant is to have God's Spirit dwelling within us, causing us to walk in his ways. How does this align with the Catholic teaching on justification that we are truly transformed?

4. What did you learn about the distinction between the Catholic view of justification and the view held by many Protestants?
   _____
   _____

5. What similarities do Catholics and Protestants have in their understanding of salvation? What are the differences in their understanding of salvation?
   _____
   _____

MEMORY VERSE

I have been crucified with Christ; it is no longer I who live, but Christ who lives in me; and the life I now live in the flesh I live by faith in the Son of God, who loved me and gave himself for me.

—Galatians 2:20

CLOSING PRAYER

May the outpouring of the Holy Spirit
cleanse our hearts, O Lord,
and make them fruitful by the inner sprinkling of his dew.
Through Christ our Lord.
Amen.
—Prayer after Communion, Votive Mass of the Holy Spirit

FOR FURTHER READING

Catechism of the Catholic Church, 1987–2029 ("Grace and Justification")

Commit—Day 1
Grace as Divine Indwelling

The *Catechism* teaches that the heart "is the dwelling-place where I am, where I live; according to the Semitic or biblical expression, the heart is the place 'to which I withdraw.' The heart is our hidden center, . . . the place of decision . . . the place of truth" (*CCC*, 2563). Jesus speaks of the "heart" as the very core of the person, where one's treasure is revealed (see Luke 6:45). Even if a person's actions appear righteous, it is the heart that defines their character.

When asked which of the commandments was the greatest, Jesus responded, "You shall love the Lord your God with all your heart, and with all your soul, and with all your mind" (Matthew 22:36–37), echoing the great *Shema* prayer of the Old Covenant (see Deuteronomy 6:4–9). God's people knew loving God with their whole hearts was necessary, but throughout salvation history they struggled to live up to this command. Dr. Barber points out that many times in Scripture God diagnoses his people with a "heart problem." They know God's commands, and they even profess the importance of keeping them, but over and over again they do not keep the Law. Their hearts stray from God.

Look up the following passages in Scripture. What do you notice about the human heart and its need for help?

Isaiah 29:13: _____

_____

Jeremiah 4:18: _____

_____

Jeremiah 5:23: _____

_____

How did man's heart become so wounded? The answer is because of sin. Not only did Adam and Eve's sin exile them from God's presence in the Garden of Eden, but their sin also shattered the beautiful integrity with which the human person was made, impairing our ability to know and choose the good (*CCC*, 418). Humanity became enslaved to sin, under sin's reign (*CCC*, 2606).

Well aware of the brokenness of mankind, God entered into a covenant with his people on Mount Sinai and gave his commands to assist his people in walking the path to life and happiness. But the Law alone was not enough. Although freed from slavery to Pharaoh, mankind was still in bondage—enslaved by something even more threatening, enslaved by sin.

SESSION 5

NOT JUST A LEGAL TRANSACTION

The Expulsion of Adam and Eve from Paradise, Benjamin West
© Everett - Art/shutterstock.com

Look up the following verses. According to Jesus, how serious is our bondage to sin?

Matthew 10:28: _____

_____

John 8:34: _____

_____

John 8:36: _____

_____

> *This kind of slavery is the worst, because it cannot be escaped from: for wherever a person goes, he carries his sin with him, even though its act and pleasure may pass: "God will give you rest from your harsh slavery (that is, to sin) to which you were subjected before" (Is 14:3). Physical slavery, on the other hand, can be escaped, at least by running away. Thus Augustine says: "What a wretched slavery (that is, slavery to sin)! A slave of man, when worn out by the harsh commands of his master, can find relief in flight; but a slave of sin drags his sin with him, wherever he flees: for the sin he did is within him. The pleasure passes, the sin (the act of sin) passes; what gave pleasure has gone, what wounds has remained." Jesus' saving work is accomplished not only by redeeming or "buying back" humanity from the debt of sin, but his work gives to humanity what they did not have before: grace and the indwelling of the Holy Spirit.*
>
> —St. Thomas Aquinas, *Commentary on the Gospel of St. John*

SESSION 5

NOT JUST A LEGAL TRANSACTION

In Jeremiah 31:31–32, God speaks of a *new covenant* that will usher in God's definitive victory over man's enslavement to sin. Look up the following Scripture passages. What do they reveal to be God's solution to the human "heart problem" and our enslavement to sin?

Deuteronomy 30:6: _____

_____

Jeremiah 31:33: _____

_____

Ezekiel 36:25–27: _____

_____

Left to our own powers, we fail. We cannot be righteous without God's help—we need God to save us from the inside out. God solves our heart problem first by saving us from sin by Christ's Death and Resurrection and then by pouring out the Holy Spirit to dwell in our hearts and be the agent of our goodness. We can be good, not of our own power, but because Christ dwells in us through the Holy Spirit and gives us *his* goodness, fulfilling what God promised to the prophet Ezekiel: that he will "cause us to walk in his ways."

Examine the following passages from the New Testament that were written to various early Christian communities to help them understand this new life in the Spirit. What will the Spirit do for us, according to these passages?

John 16:13: _____

_____

Romans 5:5: _____

_____

2 Corinthians 1:21–22: _____

_____

Though man, through his choice to sin, found himself wounded and separated from God, God in his merciful love does not abandon us, but rather forgives, heals, and makes each a new creation in Christ through the gift of the Spirit. We can rejoice with St. Paul: "Therefore, if anyone is in Christ, he is a new creation; the old has passed away, behold, the new has come" (2 Corinthians 5:17).

Commit—Day 2
Justification and the Protestant Reformation

In dialoguing with non-Catholic Christians, finding common ground and understanding each other's theological vocabulary is critical. In the matter of justification and sanctification, Protestant Christians and Catholic Christians may use some of the same words, but we may not always mean the same thing. Understanding the Scripture passages behind each other's perspective is important for fruitful dialogue.

For many Protestant Christians, particularly those who follow the Reformed tradition led by the theology of John Calvin, "justification" of the believer is understood as a strictly legal declaration. The sinful believer is declared righteous because Christ's righteousness has been imputed or given to the believer. When the believer professes faith in Christ, the believer, who is guilty, is declared righteous. Christ's innocence covers his guilt.

John Calvin, T. Woolnoth
© Georgios Kollidas/shutterstock.com

Look at Philippians 3:8–9. What might lead someone reading these verses to consider that God's righteousness does not belong to him?

_____

_____

The Protestant perspective on justification emphasizes that no man can take credit for the gift of justification. Look up Ephesians 2:8–9. What does Paul stress in these verses? Why?

_____

_____

For many Protestant Christians, focusing on the understanding that grace and righteousness belong to Christ and not to the believer protects the idea that justification is a gift and is not acquired by our own doing. Protestant Christians also want to guard against any idea that a person could add to his own glory by doing good works or trying to improve his standing before God. From their prospective, if a person did that, then he risks doing good not out of love for God but for his own benefit. For many of the Reformers, seeing justifying righteousness as not belonging in any way to the believer reinforces that Heaven is a gift.

SESSION 5

NOT JUST A LEGAL TRANSACTION

This is not to say that Protestant Christians reject the idea of transformation and sanctification. Reformed theology holds that a believer is declared *just* by God's free gift, and therefore is *saved*, freeing the believer to perform acts of charity that contribute to his sanctification freely and without the possibility of personal gain.

The Catholic view has always taught that justification is a gift and that we are totally dependent on God's grace. Some non-Catholic Christians might be surprised to know that Catholics believe justification to be "free and unmerited" (*CCC*, 1996). Rejecting any notion that we can earn the grace of justification and affirming the undeserved gift of God's grace, the Church issued this statement in 529 at the Council of Orange:

> *Canon 7. If anyone affirms that we can form any right opinion or make any right choice which relates to the salvation of eternal life, as is expedient for us, or that we can be saved, that is, assent to the preaching of the gospel through our natural powers without the illumination and inspiration of the Holy Spirit, who makes all men gladly assent to and believe in the truth, he is led astray by a heretical spirit, and does not understand the voice of God who says in the Gospel, "For apart from me you can do nothing" (John 15:5), and the word of the Apostle, "Not that we are competent of ourselves to claim anything as coming from us; our competence is from God" (2 Cor. 3:5).*

This point was reiterated at the Council of Trent at the time of the Protestant Reformation:

> *Canon 1. If anyone shall say that man can be justified before God by his own works which are done either by his own natural powers, or through the teaching of the Law, and without divine grace through Christ Jesus; let him be anathema.*

How do these quotations teach our total dependence on God for salvation?

_____
_____

At the same time that Catholic teaching proclaims that justification is a total gift of God, it also takes seriously God's expressed desire in the Old Testament to truly renew mankind from the inside. It would be difficult to view the promises to the prophets Jeremiah and Ezekiel, just to name two, without seeing God's desire for interior change and conversion.

What does Jeremiah 31:33 say about God's new covenant with his people? What might lead one to think it involves interior renewal?

_____
_____

Likewise, Jesus's own command to "be perfect as your Father in heaven is perfect" (Matthew 5:48) makes it clear that Jesus does not want his disciples to merely *appear* perfect but to actually *be perfect.* Later when speaking about how a man can be saved, Jesus states, "With men it is impossible, but not with God; for all things are possible with God" (Matthew 10:27).

The Sermon on the Mount, Carl Bloch
© wikiart.org

The primary difference between a Catholic view of justification and the Reformed Protestant view is that in the Catholic view "justification entails the *sanctification* of [one's] whole being" (*CCC*, 1995). The believer is made righteous by a gift from God so that now, having been set free from slavery to sin, they may become slaves of God (see Romans 6:20–23).

Having looked at these Scripture passages and teachings from the *Catechism of the Catholic Church* and the teachings from the Councils of Orange and Trent, we can see that the Catholic understanding in no way contradicts Philippians 3:8–9, as some non-Catholics believe. The Church recognizes and proclaims that we are dependent on God's grace, and the righteousness we have is from Christ and not by our doing. Yet, Christ's righteousness that he gives us is *truly* given to us, in order to change us from the inside. How grateful we are that his gift is so completely given that Christ's righteousness truly becomes our own by his grace.

Commit—Day 3
Lectio: "You in Me, and I in You"

In John's Gospel, during a long discourse prior to his arrest and Crucifixion, Jesus offers his disciples words of consolation: "Let not your hearts be troubled" (John 14:1). He gives one of the most direct revelations of his relationship with the Father: "If you had known me, you would have known my Father also" (John 14:7). This is not just an explanation of his own communion with the Father but an invitation for his disciples to share in that communion. Let's turn to Jesus's words of invitation and participation in the Gospel of John.

Holy Trinity, Peter Paul Rubens
© wikiart.org

> **Lectio:** The practice of praying with Scripture, *lectio divina* begins with an active and close reading of the Scripture passage. Read the verse below and then answer the questions to take a closer look at some of the details of the passage.

"Let not your hearts be troubled; believe in God, believe also in me. In my Father's house are many rooms; if it were not so, would I have told you that I go to prepare a place for you? . . . And I will ask the Father, and he will give you another Counselor, to be with you forever, even the Spirit of truth, whom the world cannot receive, because it neither sees him nor knows him; you know him, for he dwells with you and will be in you. I will not leave you desolate; I will come to you. Yet a little while, and the world will see me no more, but you will see me; because I love, you will live also. In that day you will know that I am in my Father, and you in me, and I in you. He who has my commandments and keeps them, he it is who loves me; and he who loves me will be loved by my Father, and I will love him and manifest myself to him." Judas (not Iscariot) said to him, "Lord, how is it that you will manifest yourself to us, and not to the world?" Jesus answered him, "If a man loves me, he will keep my word, and my Father will love him, and we will come to him and make our home with him."

—John 14:1–2, 16–23

SESSION 5 — NOT JUST A LEGAL TRANSACTION

In the passage, where and how does Jesus refer to a "house" or "home"?

_____

_____

How many times does Jesus refer to the Father (by name or by a pronoun)? How many times does Jesus refer to the Spirit (by name or by a pronoun)?

_____

_____

Why can't the world receive the Counselor? Why do the disciples know him?

_____

_____

What do you think Jesus meant when he said that the world will no longer see him, but his disciples will see him?

_____

_____

> **MEDITATIO:** *Lectio*, a close reading and rereading of Scripture, is followed by *meditatio*, a time to reflect on the Scripture passage and to ponder the reason for particular events, descriptions, details, phrases, and even echoes from other Scripture passages that were noticed during *lectio*. Take some time now to meditate on the above verse.

In John's Gospel, he insists on the Father who loves mankind: "God so loved the world that he gave his only Son" (Jn 3:16). And again, "if a man loves me, he will keep my word, and my Father will love him, and we will come to him and make our home with him" (Jn 14:23). Those who truly experience God's love can only repeat with ever new emotion the exclamation in John's First Letter: "See what love the Father has given us, that we should be called children of God; and so we are" (1 John 3:1). In this light, we can address God with that tender, natural, intimate name: Abba, Father. . . . Christ gives us the very life of God, a life that goes beyond time and leads us into the mystery of the Father, into his joy and infinite light.

—St. John Paul II, General Audience, September 20, 2000

SESSION 5

NOT JUST A LEGAL TRANSACTION

When Jesus is asked how he will be manifested to the disciples but not to the world, his response is that their relationship will exist in terms of love. According to Jesus, how does a person express his love for Jesus, and what is the Father's response?

_____

_____

© Oliver Denker/shutterstock.com

Jesus begins this discourse in John 14:1–2 by giving words of comfort to the disciples: "Do not let your hearts be troubled; believe in God, believe also in me. In my Father's house are many rooms; if it were not so, would I have told you that I go to prepare a place for you?" For his Jewish listeners, any reference to God's house would have caused them to think of the Temple.

God directed his people to "make me a sanctuary, that I may dwell in their midst" (Exodus 25:8) and at the dedication of the Temple we are told that "the glory of the Lord filled the house of the Lord" (1 Kings 8:11). God desired communion with his people, and so he made a way to dwell in their midst. The psalmist returns God's love: "My soul longs, yes, faints, for the courts of the Lord; my heart and flesh sing for joy to the living God" (Psalm 84:2).

The physical Temple was a preparation for God's plan to dwell among his people in his Son, the Word who was made flesh and dwelt among us (see John 1:14). As if Jesus's dwelling among us were not enough, God's plan was to include something even more marvelous. Look up 1 Corinthians 6:19. What does this passage reveal about us and where God desires to dwell?

_____

_____

SESSION 5

Jesus says that his *house* is filled with many rooms and then later that he is coming to make his *home* in us. He reveals his plan for us to be his dwelling place. How can we more readily follow God's commandments to allow the Father, Son, and Holy Spirit to make their home in us, and for us to be God's temple in our everyday lives?

_____

_____

Jesus's desire is to share his communion with the Father and the Spirit with us. Take some time to simply rest in God's love, in the mystery of the Father that Jesus desires to share with you, in the Father's joy and infinite light. Then recite the words of St. John's First Letter, making them your own: "See what love the Father has given us, that we should be called children of God; and so we are" (1 John 3:1).

> **ORATIO, CONTEMPLATIO, RESOLUTIO:** Having read and meditated on today's Scripture passage, take some time to pray, to bring your thoughts to God (*oratio*), and to be receptive to God's grace in silence (*contemplatio*). Then end your prayer by making a simple concrete resolution (*resolutio*) to respond to God's prompting of your heart in today's prayer.

COMMIT–DAY 4
TRANSFORMATIVE RIGHTEOUSNESS

In 2 Corinthians 5:17, St. Paul speaks of a "new creation." This should raise the question, "What was wrong with the old creation?" In other words, why did it need to be made new?

St. Paul explains that the source of the problem goes all the way back to Adam. Through Adam, "sin came into the world," spreading death to all men (Romans 5:12). Paul himself feels the effects of Adam's actions in his own battle to do what is good. Look up Romans 7:15–19. What is Paul's struggle? Can you relate?

_____
_____
_____

This interior battle is something with which all people have struggled. It comes as a result of the loss of God's gifts of original holiness and justice. Original justice refers to the "inner harmony" of the human person (*CCC*, 376). Adam and Eve had no strife or disorder in themselves, with others, with creation, or with God. They possessed mastery of self; their reason ordered their physical desires, their desire for earthly goods, and their self-assertion (*CCC*, 377).

This all changed with sin. When Adam and Eve rejected the sovereignty of God and disobeyed his command, they lost the gifts of original justice and original holiness. The human nature that Adam and Eve passed on to their descendants is wounded and in a fallen state. The intellect is wounded such that it no longer rightly perceives the good, and the will is wounded such that the desire for pleasure, goods, and self-assertion contends against reason.

Look up Romans 1:21–22. What does St. Paul say happened, even to man's ability to know and be truly wise?

_____
_____
_____

Humanity was grievously wounded. God in his mercy, instead of condemning man forever, set into motion the plan that would be fulfilled in Christ to bring about a *new creation*. For St. Paul and for our study on justification, it is important to see that the fall of Adam was truly universally catastrophic for mankind. Read Romans 5:19. What effect did Adam's sin have on mankind? What effect did Jesus's work have on mankind?

_____
_____
_____

Adam's offspring were not merely *declared* sinners, they actually were *made* sinners (Romans 5:19). So, when St. Paul compares Adam's sin with Christ's work of redemption, we can conclude that St. Paul understood that mankind was actually *made righteous*.

Resurrection of Christ, Raffaellino del Colle
© Claudio Giovanni Colombo/shutterstock.com

This righteousness, this new creation in Christ, is interiorly transformative, *undoing* the effects of sin. The depth of Christ's work is not superficial or merely a legal transaction. For St. Paul, we are not merely *covered* by Christ's righteousness, we are *conformed* to him. Look up the following passages to see the depth in which the life of God permeates the believer:

Romans 6:11: _____

_____

Romans 8:29: _____

_____

Galatians 2:20: _____

_____

Jesus heals humanity, saving us from sin and death, and transforming us to overcome the effects of sin, which include a weakened will, a darkened intellect, and disordered passions. Jesus's work was to transform mankind interiorly and give to him the glory that the Father desired to share with mankind from the beginning. In Adam we died, but in Christ we have new life. As St. Paul says, "He [God] is the source of your life in Christ Jesus, whom God made our wisdom, our righteousness, and sanctification and redemption; therefore, as it is written, 'Let him who boasts, boast of the Lord'" (1 Corinthians 1:30).

This transformation has a beginning (our justification), and it also involves a process of renewing our minds (Romans 12:2) and reordering our passions. Read this quote from St. John Paul II in his reflection on St. Augustine's understanding of our transformation:

> *[St. Augustine] sets forth the unutterable riches of justification - the divine life of grace, the indwelling of the Holy Spirit, and "deification" - and makes an important distinction between the remission of sins which is total, full and perfect on the one hand, and on the other hand the interior renewal which is progressive and will be full and total only after the resurrection, when the human person as a whole shares in the divine immutability.(187)*
>
> —**St. John Paul II**, *Augustinum Hipponsensem*, no. 4

Christ's work of salvation involves a process of reordering our brokenness, of conforming our will to his, so that we grow "to the measure of the stature of the fulness of Christ" (Ephesians 4:13). This transformation truly happens, but it is a process with which we participate. This understanding of our participation sets us up for the next session of this study: "Not a Spectator Sport."

Commit—Day 5
Truth and Beauty

Pentecost
Fray Juan Bautista Maíno, 1612–1614, Prado Museum, Madrid, Spain

Pentecost, Fray Jaun Bautista Maíno
© commons.wikimedia.com

Juan Bautista Maíno (1581–1649) completed this depiction of Pentecost (measuring more than nine feet tall and five feet wide) in 1614 as part of a series of four paintings for a massive altarpiece in the San Pedro Mártir Dominican Convent in Toledo, Spain, where Maíno himself took religious orders as a Domincan friar in 1613. The four paintings in the altarpiece—*The Adoration of the Shepherds*, *The Adoration of the Kings*, *Resurrection*, and *Pentecost*—portray images of the four major Christian feasts of Christmas, Epiphany, Easter, and Pentecost.

SESSION 5

NOT JUST A LEGAL TRANSACTION

The focal point of Maíno's *Pentecost* is the Holy Spirit descending as a dove, surrounded by flames of orange and gold. Before ascending into Heaven, Christ promised his disciples that he would send the Holy Spirit and told them to stay in the city "until you are clothed with power from on high" (Luke 24:49). At Pentecost, the disciples were "all together in one place. And suddenly a sound came from heaven like the rush of a mighty wind, and it filled all the house where they were sitting . . . . And they were all filled with the Holy Spirit" (Acts 2:1–4).

The Holy Spirit descends from the top of the painting on all the disciples in Maíno's *Pentecost*. They all receive God's grace, yet they all react differently. Look at the image. What reactions do you see in the faces and gestures of the disciples?

_____

_____

_____

The various reactions, positions, and gestures of the disciples serve as a reminder that God gives each person a role in the plan of salvation. Each of the disciples is unique and grace does not diminish their individuality. Rather, grace builds upon and perfects nature.

One of the most prominent figures in the painting is Mary, whom Maíno has placed, somewhat unexpectedly, not at the center but on the left side of the painting. The Holy Spirit gazes directly at our Lady, who returns his gaze. She has one hand placed over her bosom and extends her right hand down toward the Apostles around her. Her pose recalls the Annunciation, the first time she was overshadowed by the Holy Spirit. Mary was conceived immaculately, and she was saved and justified through a singular grace of God. Having received God's grace of salvation at conception, Mary cooperated with the Holy Spirit throughout her life. Her perfect reception of grace allows her to fully receive and share God's love. This ability seems to be represented by the position of her hands, both receptive of grace and extended toward others.

Below Mary, St. Peter gazes at the Holy Spirit. His whole posture is full of energy, ready to leap into action. Though his expression looks startled, his eyes are locked on the Holy Spirit and his right hand reaches to pick up the key at his feet, the symbol of his office. Opposite Peter, St. Luke is busily writing in a book, likely recording the event of Pentecost that he retells in his Acts of the Apostles. He is bent over his work, not even looking at the dove or flames, but his ear is bent toward the Holy Spirit. He responds to the promptings of the Holy Spirit with his own unique gifts. St. John the Evangelist stands behind St. Luke and peers over his shoulder at St. Luke's writing. These two Gospel writers are likely given a prominent position in Maíno's painting as a reflection of the Dominican Order's emphasis on the Word of God and preaching.

In the center of the crowd, between the evangelists and St. Peter, St. Mary Magdalene kneels in contemplative prayer. She displays yet another response to grace. She is not recording the events to share with the others, like the evangelists, or about to leap into action, like St. Peter. She is rapt in silent adoration, gazing at the Holy Spirit.

SESSION 5

Look up the following verses. What did Christ promise to the apostles and disciples?

Acts 1:4–5: _____

_____

_____

Acts 1:8: _____

_____

_____

John 14:16–17: _____

_____

_____

Maíno's altarpiece portrays major events in the life of Christ and feasts celebrated by the Church in remembrance of her Lord. In each of these events, God reveals himself to mankind. In the final portrayed event, the descent of the Holy Spirit at Pentecost, God gives the disciples the grace to participate in and continue his ministry. God invites the disciples, and each of us, into the work of salvation. Gathered together in one place, the disciples waited, and then they received the grace needed to do the work Christ appointed to them.

Take a moment to journal your ideas, questions, or insights about this session. Write down thoughts you had that may not have been mentioned in the text or the discussion questions. List any personal applications you got from the lessons. What challenged you the most in the teachings? How might you turn what you've learned into specific action?

_____

_____

_____

_____

_____

_____

_____

_____

_____

SESSION 6

NOT A SPECTATOR SPORT

OPENING PRAYER

Dear Jesus, help me to spread Thy fragrance everywhere I go. Flood my soul with Thy spirit and love. Penetrate and possess my whole being so utterly that all my life may only be a radiance of Thine. Shine through me and be so in me that every soul I come in contact with may feel Thy presence in my soul. Let them look up and see no longer me but only Jesus. Stay with me and then I shall begin to shine as you shine, so to shine as to be a light to others . . . Amen.
—Abridged from a prayer of St. John Henry Newman,
  St. Gregory's Prayer Book (Ignatius Press, 2019)

INTRODUCTION

As we continue our study, we look at how grace moves us to cooperate and participate in the work God is doing in us. This brings us to the question of the role good works play in our standing with God and our transformation as his sons and daughters. Relying heavily on Jesus's own teachings, we will see that God intends for us to make good use of the grace he gives us. God's grace moves us to do good works, and then, in his generosity, God rewards us for the good works that he gave us the grace to perform.

© addkm/shutterstock.com

Connect

Have you ever had to depend on another person in order to complete a project or task? Did you have a positive experience working with others? If so, what made it positive? If it was a negative experience, what was negative about it?

Have you ever had to learn a new skill from someone where you went from watching them perform the skill to actually performing the task yourself? What was it like when you finally mastered the skill?

Video

Watch the video segment. Use the outline below to follow along and take notes.

I. Imitation and participation
   A. Salvation is also about imitation/conformity to Christ
      1. Christ is actually living in us (Galatians 2:20)
      2. "[W]ork out your own salvation"; God is at work in us (Philippians 2:12–13)
   B. Role of works
      1. We will be judged by our works (2 Corinthians 5:10; Revelation 2:23; Matthew 25)
      2. Language of wages/earnings associated with salvation
      3. Not a contradiction of Paul's teaching (Ephesians 2:8–10)
   C. Christ in me
      1. We are Christ's Mystical Body
      2. What Christ did in his Body, he now reproduces in his Mystical Body
      3. Christ *is* the gift and he continually gives himself

SESSION 6

NOT A SPECTATOR SPORT

II. The power of grace
   A. God's work in us
      1. Grace enables us to do works that are salvific
      2. Our works are Christ's work and therefore salvific
   B. Salvation is not a spectator sport
      1. Participation is God allowing us to share in his victory
      2. Gives hope when struggling with habitual sin
   C. Saints
   D. Living like we believe it
      1. Do we despair in our sin or trust in God to help?
      2. Do we depend on prayer?

Discuss

1. For many Catholics with family or friends who are not Catholic Christians, the question of the role of works in our justification is a common point of disagreement. Did you learn anything in Dr. Barber's teaching that might help explain this issue to a non-Catholic?

2. How does St. Paul's understanding of the Mystical Body of Christ help us see not only the need for us to do good works but also Christ as the origin of our good works?

SESSION 6 — NOT A SPECTATOR SPORT

3. How do the lives of the saints illustrate that grace moves us to do good works? How do you think the saints experienced the work of grace in their lives?

   _____
   _____
   _____

4. It is important for St. Paul that "no man may boast" in his good works. It is also important that we understand our salvation to be a gift from God. How does Catholic teaching understand the need for good works but also the importance of seeing salvation as a gift?

   _____
   _____
   _____

5. What are some dangerous pitfalls that we can fall into if we neglect our dependence on God's grace on the one hand, or if we neglect the importance of our participation on the other?

   _____
   _____
   _____

Quotes, Tips, & Definitions

MERIT

The term "merit" refers in general to the recompense owed by a community or a society for the action of one of its members, experienced either as beneficial or harmful, deserving reward or punishment" (CCC, 2006).

The merit of man before God in the Christian life arises from the fact that God has freely chosen to associate man with the work of his grace. The fatherly action of God is first on his own initiative, and then follows man's free acting through his collaboration, so that the merit of good works is to be attributed in the first place to the grace of God, then to the faithful. Man's merit, moreover, itself is due to God, for his good actions proceed in Christ, from the predispositions and assistance given by the Holy Spirit (CCC, 2008).

SESSION 6 — NOT A SPECTATOR SPORT

MEMORY VERSE

For we are his workmanship, created in Christ Jesus for good works, which God prepared beforehand, that we should walk in them.

—Ephesians 2:10

CLOSING PRAYER

As we adore you, O God, who alone are holy,
and wonderful in all your Saints,
we implore your grace,
so that, coming to perfect holiness in the fullness of your love,
we may pass from this pilgrim table
to the banquet of our heavenly homeland,
through Christ our Lord.
Amen.
—Prayer after Communion, Solemnity of All Saints

FOR FURTHER READING

Michael Patrick Barber, *Salvation: What Every Catholic Should Know* (San Francisco, Greenwood Village, CO: Ignatius Press, Augustine Institute, 2019)

Nathan Eubank, *Wages of Cross-Bearing and Debt of Sin* (Berlin: De Gruyter, 2013)

Commit—Day 1
Judgment by Works

An important theme throughout these sessions is that salvation is a *gift*. God has freely justified us and given us the grace of his indwelling Spirit, making us a new creation in Christ. However, just because justification is an unmerited gift does not mean that we are not active participants in the process of being conformed to the Son.

Look up the following passages. How does Jesus intend for his disciples to demonstrate their union with him?

John 15:2: _____

_____

Mark 4:20: _____

_____

Matthew 7:18–19: _____

_____

In John's Gospel, Jesus speaks of his disciples bearing fruit precisely because they are connected to him, the vine. According to St. Paul, who is the driving force behind the work of the Christian in Philippians 2:12–13?

_____

_____

St Paul Healing the Cripple at Lystra, Karel Dujardin
© wikimedia.org

St. Paul understands obedience, right action, and the need to "work out your own salvation" in light of his understanding of "Christ who lives within me" (Galatians 2:20). St. Paul's rich theology of the Mystical Body of Christ helps us understand the relationship between how the good works of the believer truly belong to Christ (hence no man may boast) and also contribute to his or her own justification as we grow in our conformity to our Lord. For St. Paul, it is Christ's righteousness, faithfulness, and obedience that saves, and, since we are conformed to Christ through grace, the good work we do belongs to Christ and thus *also saves.*

The Conversion of St. Paul, Michelangelo da Caravaggio
© wikimedia.org

St. Paul's teaching on the unity between Christ and his people, of Christ as the Head of the Church and the Church as the Body of Christ, finds its origin in Jesus's own words to Paul at his conversion. In Acts 9:1–5, St. Paul (at this time still referred to as Saul) is blinded on the road to Damascus and confronted by the voice of the Lord, who questions, "Saul, Saul, why are you persecuting me?" Significantly, Saul never knew Jesus personally. We do know that Saul was a great persecutor of the first disciples of Christ, the early Church. How is it that Jesus states that Saul was persecuting the Lord? Because Jesus identifies the Church and its members with himself.

In St. Paul's writings, he spends a good deal of time teaching about the Church, consisting of the first believers and disciples, as the Body of Christ. What do the following passages say about the Body of Christ?

Romans 12:4–5: _____
_____
_____

SESSION 6

1 Corinthians 12:12: _____
_____
_____

Colossians 1:18: _____
_____
_____

St. Paul teaches we are actually made members of Christ's Body. In order for us to truly be conformed to Christ and act as members of his Body, we have to do what he did. For us alone, that is impossible, but with his grace, God can accomplish the impossible in us. He can transform us into the image of his Son.

St. Paul sees this transformation as involving our cooperation and participation. Grace is a gift, but we still must choose to cooperate with it, which is why St. Paul so regularly urges us in his writings to act on these graces. It is entirely possible for grace to be offered but for a person not to move his will to participate with it. This would be a foolish mistake since in the words of Jesus and the writings of St. Paul and other New Testament writers it is clear that our actions having lasting consequences on our standing before God. What do the following passages say about the effect our choices have?

2 Corinthians 5:10: _____
_____
_____

Revelation 2:23: _____
_____
_____

James 2:24–26: _____
_____
_____

This participation in our being conformed to the Son should bear itself out in our actions. What are some areas where you can cooperate with God at work in you?

_____
_____
_____

Commit—Day 2
Salvation as Compensation and the Concept of Merit

Dr. Barber has taken care to emphasize the fundamental principle that God's salvation and grace are *gifts*. Apart from God, we cannot earn our own salvation. Once we receive God's gift of salvation and decide to let his grace lead our actions, God responds to our good actions. In fact, the witness of Scripture repeatedly indicates that God wants to reward our good works.

Look up the following passages. What is the relationship between good deeds and God's reward?

Proverbs 19:17: _____
_____
_____

Daniel 4:27: _____
_____
_____

Matthew 6:4: _____
_____
_____

God's generosity and the freedom of his grace are not diminished because we participate with God's grace to do good works. Rather, our being transformed to do good works and God's reward for our good works is *part of the gift*. The *Catechism of the Catholic Church*, citing the Council of Trent, states, "The merits of our good works are gifts of the divine goodness" (*CCC*, 2009).

Throughout his teaching in the Gospels, Jesus uses financial imagery to speak of salvation. This language applies not only to the repayment of the debt of sin but also to a reward for good work. A proper translation of the original Greek text of the Scriptures assists in seeing the many places when Jesus speaks of repaying man for his good deeds. What is often translated as "reward" is actually the Greek word for "wages," *misthos*.

Look up the following passages where Jesus describes "reward," taking care to note each time the Greek *misthos* could be translated "wage" or "payment." How will God reward/repay good deeds or not repay them depending on how the person performed them?

Matthew 6:1: _____
_____
_____

SESSION 6

Matthew 6:2: _____

_____

_____

Matthew 6:4: _____

_____

_____

The words "wage" and "reward" have different connotations in contemporary English. Oftentimes "reward" is understood as a bonus for doing something that one is not expected to do, such as for finding a lost puppy. "Wage" for a job is understood in the order of justice, a financial arrangement that is agreed upon and understood by both parties. In Scripture, there is a certain sense of justice and right judgment that accompanies God's payment of good works. How does St. Paul understand God's repayment of his good works?

2 Timothy 4:7–8: _____

_____

_____

Scripture teaches that, rather than taking away God's glory or forcing his hand, God *wants* to repay our good works and actually considers it *just* to do so. St. Thomas Aquinas expressed that the reason God gave us the power to do good works is *so we would do them*. Because we participate as rational creations with a free will, God's justice seeks to repay us for our free participation in doing what he wants us to do (*Summa Theologica*, I.II.q114.a1). This is entirely consistent with the abundant generosity of God's grace and his desire to conform our will to his will, just as Jesus does.

Parable of the Workers in the Vineyard, Salomon Koninck
© wikimedia.org

SESSION 6

A key passage in Scripture that directly links work to generous repayment is the parable of the workers. In the parable of the workers in Matthew's Gospel, Jesus calls three different groups of people to labor in his vineyard. Look up the passages below and fill in the chart accordingly.

Verse	Hour the Work Began	Payment Given (see Matthew 20:8–10)
Matthew 20:1		
Matthew 20:3		
Matthew 20:5		
Matthew 20:6		

How did the first group of workers react to the repayment of the workers who came in the last hour in Matthew 20:11–12? Were they right to be upset about how the landowner distributed payment?

_____
_____
_____

How did the owner of the vineyard respond to their complaint? How does Matthew 20:13–15 describe the landowner?

_____
_____
_____

God is indeed generous with how he repays good works and this repayment is often disproportionate to the actual work done, but just as in the parable of the workers, the situation does involve *some* work on our part. We do need to work out our salvation by doing the good works God has prepared for us.

Commit—Day 3
Lectio: As You Did to the Least of These

Vienna – Jesus and Veronica
© Renata Sedmakova/shutterstock.com

The Gospel of Matthew gives us some of Jesus's most explicit teaching on salvation and the role of works. For those seeking admittance into Heaven, no clearer list of criteria is given than Jesus's words in Matthew 25, which states that we will be judged directly on our care for the hungry, thirsty, naked, sick, and imprisoned.

> Lectio: The practice of praying with Scripture, *lectio divina* begins with an active and close reading of the Scripture passage. Read the verse below and then answer the questions to take a closer look at some of the details of the passage.

SESSION 6

NOT A SPECTATOR SPORT

When the Son of man comes in his glory, and all the angels with him, then he will sit on his glorious throne. Before him will be gathered all the nations, and he will separate them one from another as a shepherd separates the sheep from the goats, and he will place the sheep at his right hand, but the goats at the left. Then the King will say to those at his right hand, "Come, O blessed of my Father, inherit the kingdom prepared for you from the foundation of the world; for I was hungry and you gave me food, I was thirsty and you gave me drink, I was a stranger and you welcomed me, I was naked and you clothed me, I was sick and you visited me, I was in prison and you came to me." Then the righteous will answer him, "Lord, when did we see you hungry and feed you, or thirsty and give you drink? And when did we see you a stranger and welcome you, or naked and clothe you? And when did we see you sick or in prison and visit you?" And the King will answer them, "Truly, I say to you, as you did it to one of the least of these my brethren, you did it to me." Then he will say to those at his left hand, "Depart from me, you cursed, into the eternal fire prepared for the devil and his angels; for I was hungry and you gave me no food, I was thirsty and you gave me no drink, I was a stranger and you did not welcome me, naked and you did not clothe me, sick and in prison and you did not visit me." Then they also will answer, "Lord, when did we see you hungry or thirsty or a stranger or naked or sick or in prison, and did not minister to you?" Then he will answer them, "Truly, I say to you, as you did it not to one of the least of these, you did it not to me." And they will go away into eternal punishment, but the righteous into eternal life.

—Matthew 25:31–46

With what titles is Jesus referred to in the Scripture passage?

_____

_____

What was the reaction of those who *did* serve the hungry, naked, sick, and imprisoned? Were they surprised by Jesus's words?

_____

_____

What were the consequences for those who did not serve the poor and marginalized?

_____

_____

> MEDITATIO: *Lectio*, a close reading and rereading of Scripture, is followed by *meditatio*, a time to reflect on the Scripture passage and to ponder the reason for particular events, descriptions, details, phrases, and even echoes from other Scripture passages that were noticed during *lectio*. Take some time now to meditate on the above verse.

SESSION 6　　　　　　　　　　　　　　　　　　　　　Not a Spectator Sport

The criterion of judgment is decisive. This criterion is love, the concrete charity to neighbour, and in particular to the "little", the people in the greatest difficult: hungry, thirsty, foreigners, naked, sick and in prison. The king solemnly declares to all that what they did or did not do to them, they did or did not do to him himself. That is to say that Christ identifies with "the least of these" his brethren, and the Last Judgment will be the account of what previously happened in earthly life. Dear brothers and sisters, it is this that interests God. Historical kingship does not matter to him; but he wants to reign in peoples' hearts, and from there, over the world: he is King of the whole universe but the critical point, the zone in which his Kingdom is at risk, is our heart, for it is there that God encounters our freedom. We, and we alone, can prevent him from reigning over us and hence hinder his kingship over the world: over the family, over society, over history. We men and women have the faculty to choose whose side we wish to be on: with Christ and his Angels or with the devil and his followers, to use the same language as the Gospel. It is for us to decide whether to practice justice or wickedness, to embrace love and forgiveness or revenge and homicidal hatred. On this depends our personal salvation but also the salvation of the world.

—Benedict XVI, Address to Pilgrims from the Southern Italian Archdiocese,
November 22, 2008

It is the heart—the center of man—that is the place where we can allow Heaven to break into our world. Alternatively, we can bar up the gates and shut out the life-giving love God wishes to give to the world. This change of heart involves shedding our selfishness and loving as God loves.

On whose side does Pope Benedict XVI say we are on if we refuse to express the love of God to others?

_____
_____
_____

Look up Luke 14:12–14. Who should the disciples avoid inviting to their banquets and parties? Who should they invite? Why?

_____
_____
_____

In what way is giving to those who cannot repay an imitation of God's generosity to us?

_____
_____
_____

Jesus is giving his disciples a very clear description of the final judgment. As Pope Benedict reflected, "[T]he critical point, the zone in which his Kingdom is at risk, is our heart, for it is there that God encounters our freedom." In what areas of your heart is God asking you to conform your will to God's will, to freely say "yes" to the good works he, the King, is calling you to do?

> **ORATIO, CONTEMPLATIO, RESOLUTIO:** Having read and meditated on today's Scripture passage, take some time to pray, to bring your thoughts to God (*oratio*), and to be receptive to God's grace in silence (*contemplatio*). Then end your prayer by making a simple concrete resolution (*resolutio*) to respond to God's prompting of your heart in today's prayer.

Commit–Day 4
The Power of Grace

In speaking about his relationship with his disciples, Jesus uses the image of the vine and the branches. Most people are familiar with the essential role a vine plays for the life of the branches: it brings life-giving water. In Jesus's use of this imagery, he is emphasizing several important facets to living life in him.

First, it is necessary to be united to him. As the Lord stated, being united to the vine is the only way the branches will survive and thrive. Union with him is necessary because salvation, that is, the ability to enter into the life of the Trinity, is impossible without him. He is the door (John 10:9) and the one true mediator (1 Timothy 2:5). Look up the following passages. What do they teach about the importance of union with Jesus Christ?

© Andrew Hagen/shutterstock.com

Matthew 19:25–26: _____

_____

1 John 4:16: _____

_____

A second important element of Jesus's teaching of the vine and the branches is that Christ's goodness and life flow through him to his disciples. Vines bring life-giving water to all the parts of the plant. Look up the following passages. How does Scripture describe the importance of this life-giving water?

John 4:14: _____

_____

Revelation 7:17: _____

_____

Revelation 22:1–2: _____

_____

The "life-giving water" is the life of grace, the life of the Spirit. Unlike a view of salvation where a person is covered with Christ's righteousness but remains interiorly untransformed, the image of the vine and the branches illustrates Christ's life permeating those united to him.

SESSION 6 — NOT A SPECTATOR SPORT

A final element of Jesus's teaching to note is that he will make those united to him fruitful, and abundantly so. The life-giving water of grace that Jesus gives flows through the believer and makes him a participant in Jesus's abundant life. What does Jesus say in John 7:38 about this grace becoming part of the believer?

_____
_____

Reflecting on John 7:38, St. Thomas Aquinas observes, "Now one who drinks natural water does not have either a fountain or a river within himself, because he takes only a small portion of water. But one who drinks by believing in Christ draws in a fountain of water; and when he draws it in, his conscience, which is the heart of the inner man, begins to live and it itself becomes a fountain" (*Commentary on John's Gospel*, 1090). Notice that for St. Thomas Aquinas the transformation of the heart is the fruit of this fountain of water. God, the source of life-giving grace, is so overflowing in his goodness that those who partake of his living water are transformed and themselves become fountains.

Christ and the Woman of Samaria at the Well, Circle of Peter Paul Rubens
© commons.wikimedia.org

At the end of the Book of Revelation, Scripture speaks again about a fountain of the water of life. This time, it pertains to the final victory God has over sin. Read Revelation 21:5–7. What does this passage say about the fountain of the water of life?

_____
_____

How does understanding the transforming power of God's grace help us overcome despair and frustration as we still battle with sin and temptation?

_____
_____

Revelation 21:7 speaks of "[h]e who conquers." What does that indicate about the importance of our participation and cooperation with God's grace?

_____
_____

In this life, we must engage in the struggle to put away our old selves and put on Christ, to live so that "[h]e must increase, but I must decrease" (John 3:30). We can see in Scripture the abundant wellspring of grace that is ours, as a free gift, for our transformation. It is given to us so that we might be united to Christ forever, that we might bear good fruit and be so full of God's grace that we ourselves become fountains of life-giving water.

Commit–Day 5
Truth and Beauty

The Charity of St. Elizabeth of Hungary
Edmund Blair Leighton, 1915, held in private collection

Charity of St. Elizabeth of Hungary, Frederic Leighton
© wikiart.org

Edmund Blair Leighton was a Victorian painter who specialized in historic genre paintings of Medieval and Regency scenes, many highly Romantic. Among his paintings is this depiction of St. Elizabeth of Hungary giving bread to the poor.

SESSION 6

St. Elizabeth was a queen in Hungary during the early 1200s. She is best remembered for her charity to the poor. In one of her most famous miracles, her husband (or, according to some sources, her brother) was displeased with her giving so much to the poor and forbade her to do so. St. Elizabeth continued to give to the poor in secret. When she went out on her missions of charity, she hid the bread under her cape. One day, her husband grew suspicious and ripped back her cloak, but instead of bread, a shower of roses fell from her cape. The king realized that St. Elizabeth was doing the work of God, asked forgiveness, and allowed St. Elizabeth to continue her charitable work.

Leighton does not depict this miracle but instead a more ordinary scene of charity. At the center of the picture, St. Elizabeth gives bread to a poor woman. They are in different postures, but both display key aspects of man's participation in God's work of salvation, receiving and giving. St. Elizabeth's humble reception of God's grace enabled her to cooperate with God in the many good works she performed for others. Having received God's grace, she shared freely so that others might also know God's love.

St. Elizabeth stands on the edge of the palace steps. She is dressed in a simple but brilliant red gown, beautifully woven with a design of gold. A slim golden crown holds her white veil in place, and a golden halo indicates the holiness of her life. Elizabeth leans out toward the poor woman and hands her a loaf of bread. Her face is calm and tranquil as she gazes at the woman she is serving. Her love of Christ, which compels her to do good works for others, shines forth in the countenance of her face.

Across from St. Elizabeth, the poor woman receives the bread. Her rough, soiled clothing contrasts with St. Elizabeth's rich robes. Her head is bent in humility and her hands are open, waiting to receive whatever St. Elizabeth gives her.

Look up the following verse. How do you see St. Paul's words illustrated in Leighton's painting of St. Elizabeth?

Ephesians 2:8–10: _____

_____

St. Elizabeth's attitude is not strained. Her posture is calm, confident in the grace of God. To the left of St. Elizabeth, there is a woman holding a large basket of bread. On the right edge of the painting, there is a crowd of people in need led by a mother, her two children, and an elderly couple. A soldier, with imperial flag in hand, stands along the castle wall. Leighton does not show the entire basket of bread, or the entire crowd, making it impossible to know if St. Elizabeth has enough bread for everyone waiting. St. Elizabeth might not know herself if she has enough bread, but this does not seem to concern her. Her confidence is in God and in doing the good works he has prepared for her. She does not strain after creating a perfect world herself, but only concerns herself with the task in front of her.

Similarly, St. Elizabeth does not wait for the poor to find her. She goes out of her castle to serve the poor she knows are there and need help. Because God has come to her, she goes to the poor. She seeks to do good works for God. She takes an active part in God's plan for salvation, for herself and those around her.

SESSION 6

Take a moment to journal your ideas, questions, or insights about this session. Write down thoughts you had that may not have been mentioned in the text or the discussion questions. List any personal applications you got from the lessons. What challenged you the most in the teachings? How might you turn what you've learned into specific action?

SESSION 7

NOT SIMPLY A MOMENT

OPENING PRAYER

God of power,
you created us in your image and likeness
and formed us in holiness and justice.
Even when we sinned against you,
you did not abandon us,
but in your wisdom chose to save us
by the Incarnation of your Son.
Open our hearts to understand your Gospel,
so that, as children of the light,
we may bear witness to your truth,
and put into practice your commands of love.
Amen.
—Adapted from RCIA prayers

INTRODUCTION

We can talk about salvation in many different ways. We can speak of it in terms of whether or not we will go to Heaven—something that is a future reality. We can also speak of a past time when we turned from a life of sin and began living for Christ, or the date on which we were baptized. In this session, Dr. Barber will examine how Scripture speaks of salvation as something that entails the past, present, and future. Understanding salvation from all these facets will help us see the full portrait of what Jesus has done for us, will do for us, and is doing in our lives to perfect us.

Sistine Chapel Ceiling, Michelangelo
© wikiart.com

Connect

How would you compare your self-confidence and self-esteem now compared to when you were a child or an adolescent? Have you found a sense of stability now as compared to your younger years?

Think of a time when you went through a really difficult period in life. When that period of trial ended, did you experience a different perspective about yourself? Did this experience change how you prioritize things that are important?

Video

Watch the video segment. Use the outline below to follow along and take notes.

I. What does it mean to be saved?
   A. Spoken of in different tenses in Scripture
      1. Past tense: "I was saved" (see Titus 3:4–7)
      2. Future tense: "I will be saved" (see 1 Corinthians 3:15)
      3. Ongoing: "I am being saved"
   B. Transformation
      1. We are to be children of God—made perfect
      2. It is impossible without God
   C. Saved *from* sin and saved *for* eternal life in God

II. Suffering and the Christian life
   A. Purifies us (Sirach 2:1–6; 1 Peter 1:6–7; 1 Corinthians 3:13–15)
      1. Demonstrates love through selflessness (Romans 5:3–5)
      2. Makes love manifest (1 Peter 4:1)
   B. Salvation is not a private affair
      1. Incorporated into Body of Christ—we suffer together (1 Corinthians 12:26; 2 Corinthians 1:6)
      2. We complete Christ's afflictions in his Mystical Body (Colossians 1:24)

SESSION 7

NOT SIMPLY A MOMENT

      3. Our suffering is redemptive because it is Christ working in his Mystical Body (Romans 12:1)

  C. Temporary punishment after death—Purgatory

      1. Perfects imperfections that remain even after death

      2. Recognizes that salvation is about being perfected

      3. Helps us become conformed to Christ who suffered for us on the Cross

DISCUSS

1. Was there anything in this session that you heard for the first time or that was an "aha" moment for you?

2. Dr. Barber spoke of salvation as not only being in the past or the future but also as being in the present tense. How do we experience salvation as an *ongoing* reality in our lives?

3. Suffering tests our faith and requires trust in God. How does suffering relate to our sanctification and relationship with Christ? How does suffering relate to love and to the building up of the Body of Christ?

4. Was there anything new you learned in Dr. Barber's teaching on Purgatory that helped you understand it better?

Quotes, Tips, & Definitions

Moved by so much suffering Christ not only allows himself to be touched by the sick, but he makes their miseries his own: "He took our infirmities and bore our diseases." But he did not heal all the sick. His healings were signs of the coming of the Kingdom of God. They announced a more radical healing: the victory over sin and death through his Passover. On the cross Christ took upon himself the whole weight of evil and took away the "sin of the world," of which illness is only a consequence. By his passion and death on the cross Christ has given a new meaning to suffering: it can henceforth configure us to him and unite us with his redemptive Passion.

—Catechism of the Catholic Church, 1505

MEMORY VERSE

But you were washed, you were sanctified, you were justified in the name of the Lord Jesus Christ and in the Spirit of our God.

—1 Corinthians 6:11

CLOSING PRAYER

May the Passion of our Lord Jesus Christ,
the intercession of the Blessed Virgin Mary, and of all the saints,
whatever good we do and suffering we endure,
heal our sins, help us to grow in holiness,
and reward us with eternal life.
Amen.
—Adapted from Rite of Penance

FOR FURTHER READING

Brant Pitre, Michael P. Barber, and John A. Kincaid, *Paul* (Grand Rapids: Eerdmans, 2019)

George T. Montague, SM, *First Corinthians: Catholic Commentary on Sacred Scripture* (Grand Rapids: Baker Academic, 2011)

Benedict XVI, Homily for Solemnity of the Assumption, August 15, 2008

Michael J. Thate, Kevin J. Vanhoozer, and Constantine R. Campbell, *"In Christ" in Paul* (Tübingen: Mohr Siebeck, 2014)

COMMIT–DAY 1
SALVATION AS BECOMING CHILDREN OF GOD

In this session, Dr. Barber shows that Scripture speaks about salvation in a multifaceted way. In speaking of salvation in different tenses, Scripture reveals a very rich portrait of the gift of abundant life God offers us in Christ.

Look up the following passages and note when salvation is received, experienced, or hoped-for in the past, present, or future.

Romans 8:24: _____
_____

Ephesians 2:8: _____
_____

Matthew 10:22: _____
_____

1 Corinthians 1:18: _____
_____

The Baptism of the Chamberlain of Queen Candace of Ethiopia, Hendrik van Balen and Jan Brueghel
© wikimedia.org

For the New Testament writers, salvation is a process. Just as after natural birth a child grows up and matures to adulthood, so too in the spiritual life there is a "birth" (John 3:5) and then we are to grow up and mature into full sonship in Christ. There is a first moment (birth), a process (spiritual maturation), and an end (entering into glory). There is a beginning of our spiritual life often associated with Baptism whereby we become sons and daughters of God. There is the ongoing maturing and growth in the spiritual and moral life as we mature in our sonship. And finally that process is to bring about our perfection when we enter into glory.

Scripture speaks of our salvation as having an identifiable beginning. Look at the following passages. In what ways is Baptism linked to aspects of salvation?

1 Corinthians 6:11: _____

_____

1 Peter 3:21: _____

_____

Titus 3:3–7: _____

_____

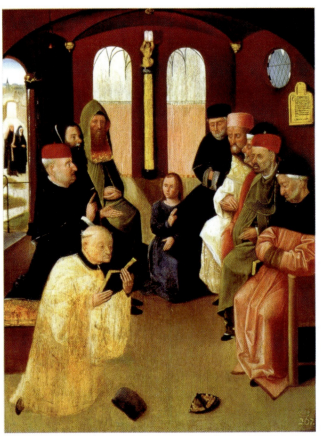

Christ's Dispute with the Doctors in the Temple, Hironymus Bosch
© wikimedia.org

SESSION 7

Not Simply a Moment

Baptism brings about the end of our old life when we were slaves to sin, and it begins our justification, sanctification, and life as a child of God in the Spirit. When we rise from the waters of Baptism, we rise to new life in Christ. Once we are conformed to the Son by our Baptism, our growing up is related to the ongoing nature of salvation, as we who are "being saved" (1 Corinthians 1:18) "work out [our] own salvation with fear and trembling" (Philippians 2:12).

Because of our Baptism, we participate in the life of Christ, who now lives in us as we grow to maturity. Baptism gave us the initial grace of adoption, but the process of sanctification entails a "workout" as we fight against the tendencies of sin that have not yet been put to death in us, and as we cooperate with the life of grace given to us in the Spirit.

What images of growth and maturity do you find in Hebrews 5:12–14?

_____

_____

Just as maturing in natural life can entail "growing pains" and trials, we also struggle as we mature in Christ. Reflect for a moment on this passage from *Veritatis Splendor*, an encyclical written by St. John Paul II, in which he discusses the difficulties in becoming fully conformed to Christ while we still battle with sin:

> *Those who live "by the flesh" experience God's law as a burden, and indeed as a denial or at least a restriction of their own freedom. On the other hand, those who are impelled by love and "walk by the Spirit" (Gal 5:16), and who desire to serve others, find in God's Law the fundamental and necessary way in which to practice love as something freely chosen and freely lived out. Indeed, they feel an interior urge—a genuine "necessity" and no longer a form of coercion—not to stop at the minimum demands of the Law, but to live them in their "fullness". This is a still uncertain and fragile journey as long as we are on earth, but it is one made possible by grace, which enables us to possess the full freedom of the children of God (cf. Rom 8:21) and thus to live our moral life in a way worthy of our sublime vocation as "sons in the Son".*
>
> —*Veritatis Splendor*, 18

There will be a time when our battle has been fought and our natural lives will end. We will stand before God, who will "render to every man according to his works" (Romans 2:6). If we persevere in love and cooperate with God's grace, we will experience the fullness of salvation when the battle in us is won and we are no longer susceptible to sin and death. At that time, we will "obtain the glorious liberty of the children of God" (Romans 8:21) and enjoy the inheritance Christ won for us—his own glory. We can look forward to "[w]hat no eye has seen, nor ear heard, nor the heart of man conceived, what God has prepared for those who love him" (1 Corinthians 2:9).

Commit–Day 2
Maturity through Redemptive Suffering

One major theme in the study so far is that salvation involves conformity to Christ. This conformity involves more than a moment—it includes growth and maturity as sons and daughters of God. Christian life means being made a new creation in Christ as he lives within us and works through us by his grace. This life in Christ and maturing in sonship manifests itself in a particular way in our lives.

Look up Romans 8:15–17. What are some important elements to life in Christ for St. Paul in this passage? What provision or caveat does Paul insist is necessary in order for us to be glorified with Christ?

_____

_____

Suffering with Christ is an indispensable part of the life of his disciples. Jesus suffered, and since he now lives in us, we can expect to also experience suffering. Jesus's suffering had very specific effects: it demonstrated his obedience to the Father, it demonstrated his love, and it brought about redemption for others. The New Testament clearly teaches that our suffering, because we are united to Christ, likewise has the same effects.

Crucifixion of Saint Andrew, Caravaggio
© wikiart.org

Two terms that are closely linked in St. Paul's thoughts are "faith" and "obedience." In Greek, the word for "faith" is *pistis*, which means far more than believing particular propositions to be true. *Pistis* is linked to faithfulness, an enduring quality, a firm and lasting commitment.

Look up the following passages. How does the meaning of faith go beyond an assent to a belief to also involve steadfastness and obedience?

Romans 1:1–7: _____

_____

James 2:19–26: _____

_____

For the New Testament writers, one's faith and faithfulness are commitments of trust in God and submission to his will, especially in the face of suffering. Faithfulness is living like Christ, who remained "obedient unto death, even death on a cross" (Philippians 2:8). Read Philippians 2:1–18. What does Paul say was in Christ and what does it mean for us to have this in mind?

_____

_____

Paul speaks of being "poured as a libation" (Philippians 2:17). He indicates Christians should imitate Christ by pouring themselves out in love for others: "Let each of you look not only to his own interests, but also to the interests of others" (Philippians 2:4). This is what it means to "work out your own salvation" because "God is at work in you" (Philippians 2:12–13).

The image Paul uses of "being poured out" makes the connection between love and suffering. What do the following passages teach about demonstrating our love for others and our love for God?

John 15:13: _____

_____

Luke 9:24: _____

_____

Matthew 16:24: _____

_____

Jesus teaches through his words and his Suffering and Death that the greatest expression of love is to lay down one's life for another. What Jesus does in his life and death is done as "one of the Trinity" (*CCC*, 470). Our imitation of Christ in our suffering is done, by the gift of grace given to us, as an imitation and participation of the Trinitarian love to which we are called. When we lay down our lives and suffer for others or endure suffering for love of God, his grace is realizing in us the Trinitarian life that constitutes the very purpose of salvation: Christ in me (Galatians 2:20).

Suffering also perfects us, purging away our attachments and imperfections. Look up the following passages and note what suffering accomplishes in those who suffer with God:

Hebrews 5:8–9: _____

_____

1 Peter 1:6–7: _____

_____

SESSION 7

1 Peter 4:1: _____
_____

1 Peter 4:12–13: _____
_____

Finally, Scripture reveals that suffering done in Christ becomes redemptive because we are united to Christ, and Christ's suffering is redemptive. How do the following passages reveal the value of suffering that is done as members of Christ's Mystical Body?

2 Corinthians 1:6–7: _____
_____

Colossians 1:24: _____
_____

Romans 12:1: _____
_____

It is hard to suffer! Whether we are suffering because we are giving ourselves in love to others, putting their needs above ours, or remaining faithful and obedient to God, suffering truly entails a denial of ourselves. It is important to remember, though, that as Jesus offered his suffering for the salvation of the whole world, our suffering as members of Christ's Mystical Body also contributes to the salvation of others. Attempting to avoid suffering not only wastes an opportunity to live in Christ but also could actually put our souls in peril of falling into selfishness and disobedience. Let us remember the words of St. Rose of Lima the next time we are faced with an opportunity to give ourselves to others and show our faithfulness to God: "Apart from the cross, there is no other ladder by which we may get to heaven" (*CCC*, 618).

St. Rose of Lima, Bartolome Esteban Murillo
© wikiart.org

Commit—Day 3
Lectio: The Stature of the Fullness of Christ

In his Letter to the Ephesians, Paul exhorts the Christians in Ephesus to recognize that God's gifts are for the unity of the faith and the building up of his Body, the Church. The gifts God gives—particularly to those who teach, evangelize, and guide others—help the whole Body grow in maturity. Let us consider Paul's words in our lives.

Biblical Ephesus Stadium
© TheBiblePeople/shutterstock.com

> **Lectio:** The practice of praying with Scripture, *lectio divina* begins with an active and close reading of the Scripture passage. Read the verse below and then answer the questions to take a closer look at some of the details of the passage.

And his gifts were that some should be apostles, some prophets, some evangelists, some pastors and teachers, to equip the saints for the work of ministry, for building up the body of Christ, until we all attain to the unity of the faith and of the knowledge of the Son of God, to mature manhood, to the measure of the stature of the fulness of Christ; so that we may no longer be children, tossed back and forth and carried about with every wind of doctrine, by the cunning of men, by their craftiness in deceitful wiles. Rather, speaking the truth in love, we are to grow up in every way into him who is the head, into Christ, from whom the whole body, joined and knit together by every joint with which it is supplied, when each part is working properly, makes bodily growth and upbuilds itself in love.

—Ephesians 4:11–16

SESSION 7 NOT SIMPLY A MOMENT

What words and images in this passage speak about the importance of unity and communion?

_____
_____

What words and images are used that speak about a lack of unity?

_____
_____

What constitutes maturity and growth?

_____
_____

What constitutes being like children?

_____
_____

> **MEDITATIO:** *Lectio*, a close reading and rereading of Scripture, is followed by *meditatio*, a time to reflect on the Scripture passage and to ponder the reason for particular events, descriptions, details, phrases, and even echoes from other Scripture passages that were noticed during *lectio*. Take some time now to meditate on the above verse.

St Paul speaks of the growth of the perfect man, who reaches the measure of the stature of the fullness of Christ. We will no longer be children at the mercy of the waves, tossed to and fro and carried about by any wind of doctrine (cf. Eph 4:13-14). "Rather, speaking the truth in love, we are to grow up in every way into him" (Eph 4:15). It is not possible to live in spiritual infancy, in an infantile faith: unfortunately, in this world of ours we see this infancy. Many have made no further progress after the first catechesis; perhaps the nucleus has remained, or perhaps it too has been destroyed. And, moreover, they are on the waves of the world and nothing else; they cannot, as adults, with skill and with profound conviction, explain and make present the philosophy of faith — so to speak — the great wisdom, the rationality of faith which also opens the eyes of others, which actually opens eyes to what is good and true in the world. Adulthood in faith is lacking and what remains is infancy in faith.
—Pope Benedict XVI, Meeting with Parish Priests of the Rome Diocese, February 23, 2012

SESSION 7

NOT SIMPLY A MOMENT

Pope Benedict XVI speaks about the dangers of our faith remaining in a state of infancy. Many passages in the New Testament speak of spiritual infancy and encourage the faithful not to remain there. How do the following passages speak about spiritual infancy and the need for maturity?

1 Corinthians 3:1–2: _____

_____

Hebrews 5:12–13: _____

_____

1 Peter 2:1–2: _____

_____

"Speaking the truth in love" is essential if we are to attain "to mature manhood, to the measure of the stature of the fulness of Christ." Speaking the truth in love is very challenging! When a person is struggling to live the Faith, it can be difficult to know what to say to help them, and it can be even more difficult to know how to say it with love. Conversely, it can also be difficult for us to receive the truth when others speak it to us.

Are there times when you found it difficult to have someone speak the truth to you? How did you react? How can you improve your reaction in the future?

_____

_____

Have you ever been in a situation where you needed to speak the truth to someone but found it challenging to say it lovingly? Was it hard for the other person to receive your desire to help them?

_____

_____

How has God shown his love and gentleness in revealing areas in your life that still need maturation and growth?

_____

_____

Recognizing the areas where we need to grow and mature requires humility. Take some time to pray the Litany of Humility, asking God for the help to grow in this virtue.

SESSION 7 — NOT SIMPLY A MOMENT

LITANY OF HUMILITY

O Jesus! meek and humble of heart, Hear me.
From the desire of being esteemed, Deliver me, Jesus.
From the desire of being loved . . .
From the desire of being extolled . . .
From the desire of being honored . . .
From the desire of being praised . . .
From the desire of being preferred to others . . .
From the desire of being consulted . . .
From the desire of being approved . . .
From the fear of being humiliated . . .
From the fear of being despised . . .
From the fear of suffering rebukes . . .
From the fear of being calumniated . . .
From the fear of being forgotten . . .
From the fear of being ridiculed . . .
From the fear of being wronged . . .
From the fear of being suspected . . .
That others may be loved more than I, Jesus, grant me the grace to desire it.
That others may be esteemed more than I . . .
That, in the opinion of the world, others may increase and I may decrease . . .
That others may be chosen and I set aside . . .
That others may be praised and I unnoticed . . .
That others may be preferred to me in everything . . .
That others may become holier than I, provided that I may become as holy as I should . . .
Amen.

> **ORATIO, CONTEMPLATIO, RESOLUTIO:** Having read and meditated on today's Scripture passage, take some time to pray, to bring your thoughts to God (*oratio*), and to be receptive to God's grace in silence (*contemplatio*). Then end your prayer by making a simple concrete resolution (*resolutio*) to respond to God's prompting of your heart in today's prayer.

_____
_____
_____
_____
_____

COMMIT—DAY 4
PURGATORY AND SALVATION

Dome of the Cathedral of Florence, Italy, Giorgio Vasari
© BlackMac/shutterstock.com

Jesus's teaching on the Sermon on the Mount not only confirms the high standards of interior perfection to which the Gospel calls us, but it also reminds us that we will face consequences if we ignore these standards. Read Matthew 5:21–26. Identify how Jesus is calling his disciples to an even greater perfection than that in the Old Testament.

_____
_____
_____
_____

What are the consequences if they fail to do this?

_____
_____
_____
_____

SESSION 7

Facade of the Chapel of Las Animas, Santiago de Compostela
© Galicia/shutterstock.com

It is jarring to think that a person could be liable to the "hell of fire" for calling a person a fool. Are there any indications that the passage refers to something other than *eternal* damnation? What does Matthew 5:26 indicate about the duration of the punishment?

_____
_____
_____

Read Matthew 18:34. Why might we understand this passage as referring to something other than the punishment of damnation?

_____
_____
_____

Jesus speaks of hell, or *gehenna*, in different ways. At times, the word *gehenna* refers to a place of *eternal* punishment (see Matthew 5:29; 18:8–9). Other times, as noted above, it refers to a place of *temporary* punishment, which is consistent with the writings of the rabbis in which *gehenna* can refer to temporary punishment.

The Old Testament speaks of the possibility of postmortem purification. The Second Book of Maccabees describes the victory that God's people won over the Greeks. Judas Maccabeus was a military leader who led a resurgence of fidelity to God and trust in his deliverance. Despite his powerful leadership, some in his company were secretly practicing idolatry. While recovering the bodies of fallen Jewish soldiers, Judas and his men discovered that some of the fallen had

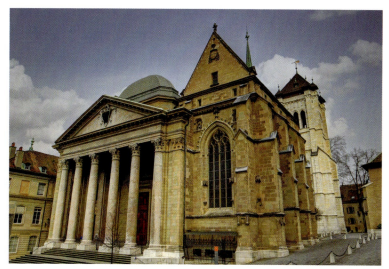

Saint Peter's Cathedral and the Chapel of the Maccabees in Geneva, Switzerland
© shutterstock.com

been carrying trinkets devoted to pagan gods. Judas and his men took to prayer "begging that the sin which had been committed might be wholly blotted out" (2 Maccabees 12:42). They also took up a sin offering on behalf of the fallen "that they might be delivered from their sin" (2 Maccabees 12:45). What do the actions of Judas and his men say about their beliefs in temporary punishment for the dead?

_____

_____

_____

If the dead had gone to a place of eternal damnation, no offering could have helped them. If they had already gone to a place of beatitude before the face of God, their offering would have been unnecessary. Judas Maccabeus's actions demonstrate that within Jewish thought there was a belief in a final purification for sins and lesser faults that remained on the soul at death, and that we on earth might assist the process of atonement by our prayers and sacrifices.

What are the ramifications of *not* believing in a final purification after death? It would be impossible to simultaneously hold the various teachings of Christ regarding salvation. If there was no opportunity for purification after death, then anyone who did not reach the standard of salvation (perfection) would not be able to enter Heaven. If God does not *really* require us to be perfect, then Jesus's teachings can be dismissed as hyperbole.

© ungvar/shutterstock.com

The natural reading of Jesus's words in Matthew 5:48, "You, therefore, must be perfect, as your heavenly Father is perfect," is that he was not exaggerating but that he *truly* meant what he said. A belief in Purgatory, a final purification to purge any remaining imperfections in those who die in God's grace and friendship, is consistent with the biblical teachings of salvation.

> *Now, we grant that even in this mortal life some punishments are purgatorial . . . they are purgatorial for those who are corrected and reformed under their constraints . . . As for temporal punishments, some suffer them only in this life, others after death, and still others both in this life and after death, but always prior to the final and most severe judgment. Nor does everyone who undergoes temporal punishments after death come under the eternal punishments which will follow that judgment. For, as we have already said, there are some for whom what is not forgiven in this world will be "forgiven in the world come." [citing Matthew 12:32]*
>
> —City of God, 21.13

Jesus teaches that the goal of discipleship is perfection, and St. Paul echoes this when he writes that we are called to "be conformed to the image of [God's] son" (Romans 8:29). This is not hyperbole. Left to our own, such a lofty calling would be impossible and lead us to despair. Jesus reminds us that "with men it is impossible, but with God all things are possible" (Matthew 19:26). The belief in Purgatory not only preserves the teaching of the New Testament that salvation involves our perfection and conformity to Christ, but this belief also requires us to recognize the need for God's grace, and to trust it.

Commit—Day 5
Truth and Beauty

The Baptism of Christ
Antoine Coypel, c. 1690, Los Angeles County Museum of Art

The Baptism of Christ, Antoine Coypel
© commons.wikimedia.org

The Baroque style of art emerged in the 1600s and was to prove a fitting instrument for the revitalization of the Catholic Faith and life in the wake of the Protestant Reformation. With its focus on drama, its use of bold colors, and its contrasting of light and shadow, many Baroque painters used this genre to instill a sense of God's grandeur and portray the beauty and truths of the Faith. Antoine Coypel's painting *The Baptism of Christ* is an exquisite example of the Roman Baroque influence in French art.

SESSION 7

Read the account of Christ's Baptism in Matthew 3:13–17. What are each of the three Persons of the Trinity doing?

_____
_____
_____
_____

The Holy Spirit, in the form of a dove, is at the center of the painting's drama. In a burst of light, reminiscent of the glory cloud that filled the Tent of Meeting and Solomon's Temple in the Old Testament, the Holy Spirit descends from the heavens, and with outstretched wings, hovers over Our Lord. Echoing the prophecy of John the Baptist's father, Zechariah, that the "day shall dawn upon us from on high to give light to those who sit in darkness" (Luke 1:78–79), the descent of God's Spirit splits the dark clouds and fills the painting with the dawn of heavenly light.

The light of the Spirit illuminates Christ and draws our attention to him. The heavenly light illuminates Jesus's skin and his brilliant royal blue robe. The manipulation of light and color that directs our gaze re-creates the workings of grace in our lives: it is by the Spirit that we know and acknowledge the Son and from the Son that our gaze is drawn back up to the Father.

Above the Spirit, the Father, with outstretched arms, looks down from Heaven. Surrounding the Trinity are representatives of the angelic choirs. The cherubic throng gaze in adoration at the members of the Trinity. The obscurity that had surrounded the Divine, represented by the wall of dark clouds, has been broken open. Man can now see the face of God and live. This relationship is supernatural, beyond man's natural capabilities. In adoring the Triune God, man joins in the worship of the angels.

Read Matthew 3:4. How is John the Baptist described?

_____
_____
_____
_____

Dressed in his coarse tunic and robe, John pours water out of a shell onto Jesus's head. While the action of his hands is at work in baptizing Jesus, John's face is turned heavenward, as he gazes toward the light of the Spirit. With the heavens opened, John sees the Spirit that consecrated him in his mother's womb (Luke 1:44) and that led him as a young man into the desert (Luke 1:80).

SESSION 7

NOT SIMPLY A MOMENT

Now look at the bottom of the painting. The waters of the Jordan River, in which Jesus stands, extend to the edge of the painting. Coypel has placed you, the viewer, in the river. You are standing in the same water that Christ is standing in, the same water he is sanctifying. To stand where you are standing you have had to come as a penitent, acknowledging your faults and failures. You have come to be baptized, to be made clean. When we see our sins, we are able to recognize Christ as our Savior. Not only are we able to see Christ as Savior, but we also see him as our model—man as he is meant to be. Wading through the water, we hope to kneel before John, to have the cleansing water poured over our heads, and to hear the words that were just addressed to Christ.

Reread Matthew 3:17. How do you feel when these words are addressed to you? Since these words *are* addressed to you, how must you live?

_____
_____
_____
_____

As a beloved child of God, we must each imitate Christ. Christ comes humbly to receive Baptism from John, "to fulfill all righteousness" and lead fallen humanity to redemption. Christ comes as the humble Son, obedient to the Spirit who will lead him into the desert to face the devil and overcome temptation. And Christ will humbly offer his life on the Cross for our salvation. The waters of our Baptism have made us sons and daughters of God. Let us go forward and imitate Our Lord.

Take a moment to journal your ideas, questions, or insights about this session. Write down thoughts you had that may not have been mentioned in the text or the discussion questions. List any personal applications you got from the lessons. What challenged you the most in the teachings? How might you turn what you've learned into specific action?

_____
_____
_____
_____
_____
_____
_____
_____
_____

SESSION 7

NOT SIMPLY A MOMENT

SESSION 8

NOT INEVITABLE

OPENING PRAYER

Hear us, Lord,
for you are merciful and kind.
In your great compassion,
look on us with love.
When we sin, may we come with confidence
before the throne of grace
to receive God's mercy,
and find pardon and strength in our time of need.
Amen.
—Adapted from Rite of Penance

INTRODUCTION

In an earlier session, Dr. Barber spoke about the misunderstanding of salvation as just "getting out of Hell." He discussed that salvation is so much more than "fire insurance." Why then is it necessary to speak of Hell in a discussion of salvation? While Jesus spent a great deal of time proclaiming the "good news" of salvation, he also warned his disciples of an "eternal fire" (Matthew 25:41). Salvation is a gift, but how does our free will and the choices we make affect our salvation?

© Khakimullin Aleksandr/shutterstock.com

Connect

Have you ever given a gift that you felt obligated to give? How did that affect your feelings about giving it compared to when you gave a gift freely?

Have you ever had a challenge in a friendship that was so severe that the relationship just could not continue?

Video

Watch the video segment. Use the outline below to follow along and take notes.

I. Hell
   A. Feature of Jesus's teachings
      1. Matthew 25—sheep and the goats
      2. Matthew 7:21—"Not every one . . . shall enter the kingdom of heaven"
      3. Luke 13:24—"Many . . . will seek to enter and will not be able"
   B. Eternal punishment, affects soul and body (John 5:28–29; Revelation 14:11)
   C. Prolonged suffering
      1. Not annihilation
      2. Torment day and night forever
   D. Sins that demonstrate a rejection of God
      1. There are sins that, if left unrepented, bar one from Heaven (1 Corinthians 6:9–11)
      2. Not contradictory to God's love
II. Sin is a human choice
   A. God respects our choices
   B. Humans have the ability to make choices that last (Deuteronomy 30:15; Isaiah 66:3–4; Sirach 15:15; Revelation 2:5)
III. Once saved, always saved? (Romans 8:35–39)
   A. Sin can separate us from the love of Christ (1 Corinthians 4, 15; John 15)
      1. We can choose to reject him
      2. It is possible to believe in vain if we do not persevere
   B. The vine and the branches

SESSION 8

C. Mortal sin (1 John 5:16–17)
   1. Mortal sin: grave matter, full knowledge, full consent
   2. Restored through the Sacrament of Confession (James 5)
IV. Prayer—need to stay close to Jesus Christ (*CCC*, 2744)

Discuss

1. What stood out to you as something new you learned in this session? Were there any "aha" moments?

   _____
   _____
   _____

2. How does God regard man's ability to choose for himself? Is it surprising that God truly respects our choices—even if we make choices that are contrary to his will?

   _____
   _____
   _____

3. Why is perseverance in our faith and avoiding serious sin so important if we wish to be saved?

   _____
   _____
   _____

4. What are the three conditions that must be met in order for a sin to be considered a *mortal sin*. How must we properly repent of mortal sin in order to the restore God's life in us?

   _____
   _____
   _____

5. Do you experience difficulties in finding time to pray? How does the *Catechism*'s quotation of St. Alphonsus Liguori ("Those who pray are certainly saved . . .") provide encouragement?

_____
_____
_____

MEMORY VERSE

Not every one who says to me, "Lord, Lord," shall enter the kingdom of heaven, but he who does the will of my Father who is in heaven.

—Matthew 7:21

CLOSING PRAYER

Lord Jesus Christ, most merciful Saviour of the world,
we humbly beseech You, by Your most Sacred Heart,
that all the sheep who stray out of Your fold
may one day be converted to You,
the Shepherd and Bishop of their souls,
who lives and reigns with God the Father
in the unity of the Holy Spirit, world without end.
Amen.
—Prayer for the Conversion of Sinners

FOR FURTHER READING

C.S. Lewis, *The Great Divorce* (Harper One: New York, 1973)

Robert Bellarmine, *Hell and Its Torments* (Tan Books: Charlotte, NC, 1990)

Ralph Martin, *Will Many Be Saved?* (Eerdmans: Grand Rapids, MI, 2012)

Catechism of the Catholic Church, 1033–1037 ("Hell") and 2742–2745 ("Persevering in Love")

COMMIT–DAY 1
"For Many Will Seek to Enter and Will Not Be Able"

The Last Judgement, Jean Cousin
© wikimedia.org

Scripture clearly teaches about God's love and goodness, as well as his desire for "all men to be saved" (1 Timothy 2:4). Yet many passages clearly teach that despite God's desire for our salvation, not all will be saved. What in the following passages indicates that not all will enter the Kingdom of Heaven?

Matthew 7:21–23: _____

_____

Matthew 25:41: _____

_____

Revelation 20:10: _____

_____

These are sobering passages, especially Matthew 7:21–23, which shows that some who think that they will enter the Kingdom will be told to depart from Christ. Why do they think they should be welcomed into the Kingdom? What will constitute their failure to enter?

_____

_____

153

SESSION 8

NOT INEVITABLE

The Crucifixion, The Last Judgment, Jan van Eyck
© Everett - Art/shutterstock.com

In the previous session we looked at passages where *gehenna* referred to something other than eternal damnation. Yet there are clearly passages in the Gospels where it does refer to everlasting punishment. In some passages Jesus indicates that there could be a release from the "hell of fire" if a person committed certain sins. There are other passages in which Jesus explicitly speaks of *gehenna* as a place of eternal punishment.

What do the following passages say about a place of permanent or eternal punishment?

Matthew 18:8–9: _____

_____

Matthew 10:28: _____

_____

Many struggle with the biblical passages about Hell, but to fail to consider the reality of eternal punishment for those who reject God is to ignore Jesus's own words. The plain meaning of Jesus's teaching is that Hell exists and that it will not be unpopulated. Look at the following passages. How does Jesus underscore the reality of eternal damnation?

Luke 13:24: _____

_____

Mark 14:21: _____

_____

SESSION 8

NOT INEVITABLE

In addition, the New Testament clearly teaches that eternal damnation is never ending and that it also involves a physical component. How can these truths be found in the following passages?

Matthew 10:28: _____
_____
_____

John 5:28–29: _____
_____
_____

The Last Judgment, Cathedral of Florence.
Giorgio Vasari/ Federico Zuccaro
© Conde/shutterstock.com

Heavenly glory entails our sharing in Christ's glory both spiritually and physically, body and soul. Conversely, damnation also entails both spiritual and physical torment. In Heaven, joy is found in perfect union with God. In Hell, eternal separation from God is the severest punishment we face (*CCC*, 1035).

Jesus's teaching that some will not enter into his kingdom is sobering. It entails a call for each of us to be vigilant in our rejection of evil—the stakes could not be higher. The life of grace is a share in the life and love of the Trinity. Sin is the antithesis of this love and is therefore in opposition to our share in eternal life.

See the following passages. What do they teach about sin's incompatibility with God's life?

1 John 3:14–15: _____
_____

Romans 2:7–8: _____
_____

Ephesians 4:17–23: _____
_____

Our recognition of Hell and a right fear of punishment can help us to avoid evil and lead us to repentance. Nevertheless, what should ultimately motivate us is not fear of punishment but love of God. To simply speak of salvation in terms of what we are saved *from* is to miss out on the greatest part of the Good News: that we are called to enter into God's own life of love. Yes, by our sin we merit Hell. But God calls us into something so wondrous: "What no eye has seen, nor ear heard, nor the heart of man conceived, what God has prepared for those who love him" (1 Corinthians 2:9). Thankfully, God gives us the grace to turn from sin and obtain eternal life with him.

Commit—Day 2
Mortal Sin and Severing Oneself from Christ

After a person has received the gift of grace and initial justification, can he or she be separated from Christ by sin? Many non-Catholic Christians hold that a person *cannot* be separated from Christ after receiving the gift of justification, that once a person has been saved, according to those who hold to eternal security, he cannot lose his salvation—"once saved, always saved."

A key passage used in support of the concept of eternal security is Romans 8:38–39. What might lead a person to think this passage guarantees salvation under every circumstance?

_____

_____

Context is important in a proper understanding of this passage. If we back up a couple verses to Romans 8:35–37, we see that Paul's audience is experiencing persecution. They are being killed and regarded as sheep to be slaughtered. Paul's message is that their persecutors might kill the body, but there is nothing that others can do that will separate them from Christ and the love of God.

The Last Judgment, Joos van Cleve
© Everett - Art/shutterstock.com

But Paul does not teach that *sin* cannot separate us from Christ in this passage or anywhere else in his writings. In fact, Paul spoke of constant vigilance with regard to one's own salvation and right-standing before God, and he admonished believers to guard against presumption in their own salvation. How do the following passages communicate the importance of perseverance and ongoing faithfulness? What is the consequence for those who depart from Christ's teachings and turn away from living the Christian life?

1 Corinthians 4:4–5: _____

1 Corinthians 9:27: _____

Galatians 5:4: _____

Romans 11:22: _____

1 Timothy 1:19: _____

Hebrews 4:1: _____

Paul's teaching, and in particular his language about being "cut off" in Romans 11:22, echoes the teachings of Jesus in the Gospels. Jesus spoke about the importance of abiding in him and the consequences if we choose not to abide in him: "If a man does not abide in me, he is cast forth as a branch and withers; and the branches are gathered, thrown into the fire and burned" (John 15:6). These passages reveal that it is possible to be cut off and "cast into the fire," even for those who were once connected to Christ.

Since God is always faithful and desires our salvation, it is not *God* who cuts us off from the life of grace. Rather, it is us who sever our selves from Christ by our own choosing of sin, particularly mortal sin. Venial sin wounds the life of grace dwelling within us, moral and mortal sin extinguishes that eternal life. How do the following passages describe the relationship between sin and death?

Romans 6:16: _____

James 1:15: _____

1 John 5:16–17: _____

When we commit sin, we are turning away from God and not living as true sons and daughters. Some sins are so serious that by willingly committing them and having full knowledge of their gravity, we are purposefully rejecting the life of grace and sonship in Christ that God is giving us.

The *Catechism of the Catholic Church* explains that certain sins—called venial sins—weaken our love for God and incline us toward more serious sin if we fail to repent, but venial sins themselves do not extinguish sanctifying grace within us (*CCC*, 1863). On the other hand, there are sins—called mortal sins—that destroy the charity in our hearts and the sanctifying grace that gives us eternal life. For a sin to be considered mortal, the object of our sin must entail grave matter, and we must have committed it with full knowledge and full consent.

Mortal sin is a radical possibility of human freedom—as is love itself. Mortal sin results in the loss of charity and the privation of sanctifying grace, that is, of the state of grace. If it is not redeemed by repentance and God's forgiveness, it causes exclusion from Christ's Kingdom and the eternal death of Hell, for our freedom has the power to make choices, the consequences of which extend to eternity.

Church of St Augustine in Victoria, Gozo Island, Malta
© Gergana Encheva/shutterstock.com

Thanks be to God, the life of grace can be restored by a conversion of heart imploring God's mercy through the Sacrament of Confession (*CCC*, 1856).

> *While he is in the flesh, man cannot help but have at least some light sins. But do not despise these sins which we call "light": if you take them for light when you weigh them, tremble when you count them. A number of light objects makes a great mass; a number of drops fills a river; a number of grains makes a heap. What then is our hope? Above all, confession.*
>
> —St. Augustine, Homily on the First Epistle of John

The habit of regular Confession, a daily prayer life, and vigilance in growing in the virtues will help us to not only avoid mortal sin but also to overcome venial sin so that we might "be zealous to be found by [Christ] without spot or blemish, and at peace" (2 Peter 3:14).

Commit—Day 3
Lectio: Building on the Rock

Jesus concludes his Sermon on the Mount (Matthew 5–7) with very serious words warning against self-deception, and exhorting his audience to not be hearers only but to also put into action the teachings they have just heard.

> **Lectio:** The practice of praying with Scripture, *lectio divina* begins with an active and close reading of the Scripture passage. Read the verse below and then answer the questions to take a closer look at some of the details of the passage.

"Not every one who says to me, 'Lord, Lord,' shall enter the kingdom of heaven, but he who does the will of my Father who is in heaven. On that day many will say to me, 'Lord, Lord, did we not prophesy in your name, and cast out demons in your name, and do many mighty works in your name?' And then will I declare to them, 'I never knew you; depart from me, you evildoers.' Every one then who hears these words of mine and does them will be like a wise man who built his house upon the rock; and the rain fell, and the floods came, and the winds blew and beat upon that house, but it did not fall, because it had been founded on the rock. And every one who hears these words of mine and does not do them will be like a foolish man who built his house upon the sand; and the rain fell, and the floods came, and the winds blew and beat against that house, and it fell; and great was the fall of it." And when Jesus finished these sayings, the crowds were astonished at his teaching, for he taught them as one who had authority, and not as their scribes.

— Matthew 7:21–29

Do you think those who will be told to depart from Christ will be surprised at Jesus's words to them?

_____
_____

Why did Jesus call the wise man wise? What did he do in contrast to the foolish man?

_____
_____

Both types of men (the foolish and the wise) experienced rain, floods, and winds. What do you think these catastrophes represent for Jesus's followers?

_____
_____

> **MEDITATIO:** *Lectio*, a close reading and rereading of Scripture, is followed by *meditatio*, a time to reflect on the Scripture passage and to ponder the reason for particular events, descriptions, details, phrases, and even echoes from other Scripture passages that were noticed during *lectio*. Take some time now to meditate on the above verse.

My friends, this brings about a question: "How do we build this house?" Without doubt, this is a question that you have already faced many times and that you will face many times more. Every day you must look into your heart and ask: "How do I build that house called life?" Jesus, whose words we just heard in the passage from the evangelist Matthew, encourages us to build on the rock. In fact, it is only in this way that the house will not crumble. But what does it mean to build a house on the rock? Building on the rock means, first of all, to build on Christ and with Christ. Jesus says: "Every one then who hears these words of mine and does them will be like a wise man who built his house upon the rock" (Mt 7:24). These are not just the empty words of some person or another; these are the words of Jesus. We are not listening to any person: we are listening to Jesus. We are not asked to commit to just anything; we are asked to commit ourselves to the words of Jesus.

To build on Christ and with Christ means to build on a foundation that is called "crucified love". It means to build with Someone who, knowing us better than we know ourselves, says to us: "You are precious in my eyes and honoured, and I love you" (Is 43:4). It means to build with Someone, who is always faithful, even when we are lacking in faith, because he cannot deny himself (cf. 2 Tim 2:13). It means to build with Someone who constantly looks down on the wounded heart of man and says: "I do not condemn you, go and do not sin again" (cf. Jn 8:11). It means to build with Someone who, from the Cross, extends his arms and repeats for all eternity: "O man, I give my life for you because I love you." In short, building on Christ means basing all your desires, aspirations, dreams, ambitions and plans on his will. It means saying to yourself, to your family, to your friends, to the whole world and, above all to Christ: "Lord, in life I wish to do nothing against you, because you know what is best for me. Only you have the words of eternal life" (cf. Jn 6:68). My friends, do not be afraid to lean on Christ! Long for Christ, as the foundation of your life! Enkindle within you the desire to build your life on him and for him! Because no one who depends on the crucified love of the Incarnate Word can ever lose.

—Pope Benedict XVI, Address to the Young People in Poland, May 2006

The verses of our *lectio* passage conclude Jesus's Sermon on the Mount. Look at the following verses from earlier in this sermon. What are some of the radical teachings of "crucified love" that Jesus is calling us to live out?

Matthew 5:28: _____

Matthew 5:41: _____

Matthew 5:44: _____

SESSION 8

NOT INEVITABLE

The Sermon on the Mount, Carl Bloch
© wikiart.org

Whether we are judged to be wise or foolish depends on what we "do." Both the wise and the foolish hear Jesus's teaching, but only the wise put Jesus's teaching into action. Look up James 2:14–19. How does James echo this teaching of Jesus?

_____
_____

Jesus speaks of the one "who does the will of my Father." Pope Benedict XVI repeats the phrase "to build with Someone" several times in his reflection. Take some time to review "all your desires, aspirations, dreams, ambitions and plans." Are they based on God's will? If not, what can you do to begin to conform them to the will of God?

_____
_____

> ### Oratio, Contemplatio, Resolutio:
> Having read and meditated on today's Scripture passage, take some time to pray, to bring your thoughts to God (*oratio*), and to be receptive to God's grace in silence (*contemplatio*). Then end your prayer by making a simple concrete resolution (*resolutio*) to respond to God's prompting of your heart in today's prayer.

_____
_____
_____

Commit—Day 4
Taking Oneself to Hell

God made us with the ability to control our own actions so that we might seek him of our own accord (*CCC*, 1730). St. Irenaeus states, "Man is rational and therefore like God; he is created with free will and is master over his acts" (*Against Heresies*). God gave man the power to exercise his freedom, making man responsible for his own acts (*CCC*, 1745).

Consider the following passages. What do they indicate about man's ability to make his own choices?

Deuteronomy 30:19: _____

_____

Sirach 15:15: _____

_____

St. John Paul II, in his General Audience (January 16, 1980), teaches that this freedom is given to man so that he might make a "sincere gift of himself" to "fully discover his true self." This gift of self is in imitation of Christ, who "emptied himself" (Philippians 2:7) for our salvation. This self-emptying expresses in Jesus's humanity the divine love of the Trinity (*CCC*, 470). Jesus is the model for how we are to live as sons and daughters of God, and the gift of grace is the means by which this life is possible. We are called to imitate Christ by freely making ourselves a gift.

God desires that we use our freedom to make this gift and live in Christ. Yet because God gave man the ability to authentically make his own choices, some people may choose not to make a gift of themselves and instead may abuse their freedom.

What do the following passages teach about the proper use of our freedom?

Galatians 5:13: _____

_____

_____

1 Peter 2:16: _____

_____

_____

SESSION 8   NOT INEVITABLE

Before becoming Pope, Benedict XVI described the intersection of God's gift of salvation and man's freedom, saying:

> *A second point to add to this is that God never, in any case, forces anyone to be saved. God accepts man's freedom. He is no magician, who will in the end wipe out everything that has happened and wheel out his happy ending. He is a true father; a creator who assents to freedom, even when it is used to reject him. That is why God's all-embracing desire to save people does not involve the actual salvation of all men. He allows us the power to refuse.*
> —Joseph Ratzinger, *God Is Near Us: The Eucharist, the Heart of Life*

One might reasonably question, who would refuse salvation? Who would willingly make choices that lead to Hell? Its description is so ghastly and undesirable, it would seem that no person would freely choose it.

In his Sermon on the Mount, Jesus himself gives us some insight into the choice, ". . . for the gate is wide and the way is easy, that leads to destruction, and those who enter by it are many. For the gate is narrow and the way is hard, that leads to life, and those who find it are few" (Mathew 7:13–14). The way that leads to life is not easy and, as a result, many do not make the choice for eternal life.

As Dr. Barber emphasizes in this study, salvation is not merely about becoming "a good person" or a "better you." We are called to perfection. Following the path to Christ's glory in us means we need to "put to death . . . what is earthly in you: immorality, impurity, passion, evil desire, and covetousness, which is idolatry" (Colossians 3:5). This is hard and needs a firm commitment to God, over and above our self.

The battle we must fight to be transformed to Christ is difficult. It feels like a death to ourselves. It takes discipline, humility in our failures, and saying no to our disordered desires. It requires suffering and laying down our lives for others. Jesus was up-front with his disciples about the trials involved in following him. How did Jesus describe the life of discipleship?

Matthew 10:38: _____

_____

Matthew 24:9: _____

_____

Luke 14:27: _____

_____

Jesus spoke regularly of doing the will of his Father. In his own life, Jesus perfectly followed his Father's will, accepting "even death on a cross" (Philippians 2:8). Jesus's Crucifixion exemplifies how we are to pour ourselves out in love for the Father, give of ourselves for the sake of others, prefer God's will to our own, and prefer faithfulness to God even above our own life. The Cross shows us what it looks like for a human to love as God loves. Understandably—at least on a natural level—most people would not choose this radical self-emptying love. Only with God's help can we make such a gift of ourselves.

The Virgin at Prayer, Metsys
© wikiart.org

Trusting God enough to give ourselves to him and to his will requires a deep personal friendship that only grows by a life defined by prayer. Consider the following passage from the *Catechism of the Catholic Church*.

> **Prayer is a vital necessity.** *Proof from the contrary is no less convincing: if we do not allow the Spirit to lead us, we fall back into the slavery of sin. How can the Holy Spirit be our life if our heart is far from him? Nothing is equal to prayer; for what is impossible it makes possible, what is difficult, easy. . . . For it is impossible, utterly impossible, for the man who prays eagerly and invokes God ceaselessly ever to sin. Those who pray are certainly saved; those who do not pray are certainly damned.*
>
> —*Catechism of the Catholic Church*, 2744

Prayer is the foundation of our relationship with God. Like any friendship, it is nourished by time spent together where we converse often and at length. Christ sees us as his friends (John 15:13), and we can reciprocate that love and friendship and undertake—with his help—the demands of discipleship. We need to prioritize prayer so that when we suffer or are tempted, we can remain firmly rooted to Christ and lay down our lives for him in love and friendship.

Commit—Day 5
Truth and Beauty

Vault Mosaics
Baptistery of St. John, Florence, Italy, ca. 1225–1330

Vault Mosaics, Bapistery of John, Florence, Italy
© wjarek/shutterstock.com

The Baptistery of St. John stands next to the Florence Cathedral in the Piazza del Duomo in Florence, Italy. This octagonal baptistery was built in the eleventh century over the site of an earlier baptistery from the fourth or fifth century, which itself was likely built over a more ancient building, possibly a Roman pagan temple that had been converted into a church. A baptistery is a separate building built for the administration of the Sacrament of Baptism.

Magnificent golden mosaics cover the entire interior surface of the octagonal dome. These ceiling mosaics took nearly 100 years to complete, with work beginning around 1225 and continuing roughly until 1330.

Upon entering the baptistery, one's attention is immediately drawn upward to the glimmering gold that crowns the building. The dome's artwork is dominated by a huge figure of Christ in Judgment, which entirely fills one of the octagonal sections over the altar. The two octagonal sections to Christ's left and right contain three parallel registers in which are seen angels (who carry instruments of Christ's Passion), then the Virgin Mary, the Apostles (holding books

Baptistery of Florence, view of the mosaic ceiling
© wjarek/shutterstock.com

written in various languages, reflecting their work of evangelization to the whole world), and other saints, and on the lowest register are scenes of the Last Judgment. Christ is surrounded by a circular mandorla, or frame, a symbol of heavenly glory. He sits on a stylized version of a rainbow throne that recalls John's vision in Revelation 4:3 of a rainbow around the throne of God.

Jesus's feet and hands retain the marks of the Crucifixion. Jesus extends his hands to the left and right toward the scenes of the Last Judgment just below him, but the position of each palm is different. Recalling the parable of the sheep and goats in Matthew 25, Christ's right hand is positioned with the palm up as he welcomes into heavenly glory those who have been saved by the blood of the Lamb and who cooperated with God's grace as it transformed them. These people see Christ as their highest happiness. They joyously climb out of their tombs to share eternity with Christ.

In contrast, Christ's left palm faces downward toward those who have rejected him. Rather than giving themselves to Christ, they chose to give themselves to their own desires. These are ripped out of their tombs by hideous demons. Christ did not force them to choose his life. He respects their free will, and his downward facing left palm indicates that he will not allow them into his presence, respecting their own choosing.

On the remaining sections of the octagonal dome, concentric circles depict numerous scenes. From the top of the dome moving downward these include ornamental motifs, the hierarchies of angels with Jesus, narrative stories from the Book of Genesis, stories of the patriarch Joseph, stories of the Virgin Mary and Christ, and finally stories of the baptistery's patron, St. John the Baptist.

SESSION 8

The baptistery's gold background is a convention taken from Byzantine iconography and represents Christ's eternal glory. It is the glory that Christ invites each person to share in: the glory that awaited each person who received Baptism in this baptistery. In all its shimmering glory, the mosaic dome—with its narrative images from salvation history—proclaims the grand story of salvation into which the newly baptized have now entered. And with its primary image of Christ in Judgment, it calls the newly baptized to not take for granted the gift they had just received, but rather to come to full maturity in Christ their Lord.

Paul speaks about the proper use of freedom for service of others and the misuse of freedom for the flesh (see Galatians 5:13–15). All of the saints that are depicted on either side of Christ made use of their freedom for service. They subjected the desires of the flesh to the goods of the Spirit. Directly on Christ's right hand is Mary, who accepted the Christ Child into her womb and any scorn that may have accompanied the unexpected pregnancy. Next to Mary is Peter, who left everything he once knew for Christ and ultimately accepted martyrdom. On Christ's left side is St. John the Baptist, who left the comforts of life to live in the desert and witness to the coming of the Messiah, ultimately accepting death himself for Christ. Above the saints, angels carry the instruments of Christ's Passion. The Cross, crown of thorns, chalice, and other instruments remind the viewer that Christ used his freedom and power for love, willingly sacrificing himself for our salvation, and still bears the wounds of his gift of self on his glorified body.

Even when Christ sits as judge upon his heavenly throne, he still bears the marks of his love and mercy for all mankind. The Baptistery of St. John, with its golden vault mosaics, is wonderful to behold, but even more glorious is the truth of God's saving love that its images proclaim to all who enter its doors.

Take a moment to journal your ideas, questions, or insights about this session. Write down thoughts you had that may not have been mentioned in the text or the discussion questions. List any personal applications you got from the lessons. What challenged you the most in the teachings? How might you turn what you've learned into specific action?

_____
_____
_____
_____
_____
_____
_____
_____
_____
_____

SESSION 8

NOT INEVITABLE

SESSION 9

NOT JUST FOR OTHER PEOPLE

OPENING PRAYER

Father of mercy,
you led the man born blind
to the kingdom of light
through the gift of faith in your Son.
Free us from the false values that surround and blind us.
Set us firmly in your truth,
children of the light for ever.
We ask this through Christ our Lord.
Amen.
—Adapted from RCIA prayers

INTRODUCTION

In this session, we will look at one of the biggest obstacles in the spiritual life: ourselves. God is eager to forgive us of our sins and give his grace to conform us into the image of his Son, but in order to receive forgiveness, we must repent! Repenting of our sin means taking responsibility for our failures and admitting that we struggle to love God from the heart. How can we practice more readily recognizing our sin and asking for God's help and the help of those God has put in our lives?

© No-Te Eksarunchai/shutterstock.com

Connect

Have you ever found it easy to notice the fault in another person and later have it dawn on you that you struggle with the same thing? How did that make you feel when you came to this realization?

Has anyone ever told you about something you were doing wrong? How did you react? Why is it difficult to be told you need to improve on something?

Video
Watch the video segment. Use the outline below to follow along and take notes.

I. Implications of speaking of salvation
   A. Discomfort speaking about *our* sin and *our* need for a savior
      1. Mary refers to God as "my Savior"
      2. We recognize our own sinfulness and our need for salvation
   B. Parable of the Pharisee and the tax collector (Luke 18:9–14)
      1. Pharisees often misunderstood
      2. We need humility
      3. Need to focus on our own sins more than others' sins

II. Christ reveals man to himself
   A. Must be born *anothen* (John 3:1–21)
      1. *Anothen* can mean "again" or "from above"
      2. Nicodemus struggles to understand because of his concern with earthly things
      3. Jesus's words reveal what is important to us and how our culture has shaped us
   B. Baptism transforms man to be born from above

III. Called to transformation
   A. Sacraments and prayer
   B. Renewal of our mind (Romans 12:2)
   C. Ongoing conversion
   D. Studying our faith

SESSION 9   NOT JUST FOR OTHER PEOPLE

DISCUSS

1. What is something that struck you in this session? Did you learn something new?
   _____
   _____
   _____

2. How is the parable of the Pharisee and the tax collector an important lesson for us as we grow in our faith?
   _____
   _____
   _____

3. How does recognizing our need for a savior and salvation help us honestly confront the areas in our lives that need transformation?
   _____
   _____
   _____

4. Christ reveals man to himself. How did Jesus's words to Nicodemus reveal Nicodemus's worldly thinking?
   _____
   _____
   _____

5. Why is it important to study our faith?
   _____
   _____
   _____

QUOTES, TIPS, & DEFINITIONS

Jesus calls to conversion. This call is an essential part of the proclamation of the kingdom: "The time is fulfilled, and the kingdom of God is at hand; repent, and believe in the gospel." In the Church's preaching this call is addressed first to those who do not yet know Christ and his Gospel . . . . Christ's call to conversion continues to resound in the lives of Christians . . . . This endeavor of conversion is not just a human work. It is the movement of a "contrite heart," drawn and moved by grace to respond to the merciful love of God who loved us first.

—Catechism of the Catholic Church, 1427–1428

MEMORY VERSE

Again Jesus spoke to them, saying, "I am the light of the world; he who follows me will not walk in darkness, but will have the light of life."

—John 8:12

CLOSING PRAYER

O Holy Spirit, enlighten me and help me now to know my sins as one day I shall be forced to recognize them before thy judgment seat. Bring to my mind the evil which I have done and the good which I have neglected. Call to my mind the ways in which I have not lived in alignment with thy love for me and with my identity as your beloved adopted child. Permit me not to be blinded by self-love. Grant me, moreover, heartfelt sorrow for my transgressions, and the grace of a sincere confession, so that I may be forgiven and admitted into thy friendship.
—Adapted from a Prayer Before Confession

FOR FURTHER READING

Francis de Sales, *Introduction to the Devout Life*

Ralph Martin, *The Fulfillment of All Desire* (Steubenville: Emmaus Road Publishing, 2006)

Josemaria Escrivá, *The Way* (Image, 2006 reprint edition)

COMMIT–DAY 1
You Are Spiritually Blind . . . Yes, You!

The contrast between *light* and *darkness* is found throughout Scripture. In the opening chapter of Genesis, one of God's first creative acts is to illumine the world (Genesis 1:3). In the Exodus, God accompanies his people as a pillar of fire and light (Exodus 13:21), and God instructs Moses to keep a lamp burning continually in the Tent of Meeting, where God's presence dwells (Exodus 27:20–21).

But the creative act of bringing light out of darkness pales in comparison to the work that God wants to accomplish in our hearts, freeing us from the darkness of sin with the light of his love. Look up the following passages and note how God uses light and darkness to refer to good and evil.

Psalms 43:3: _____

Proverbs 4:19: _____

John 3:19: _____

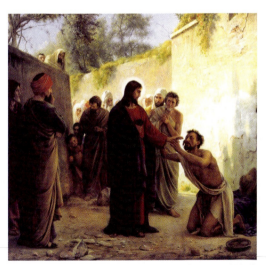

Healing of the Blind Man, Carl Bloch
© commons.wikimedia.org

Something we encounter in Scripture—and in our own lives—is the possibility of not realizing our own spiritual blindness. In John 9:1–41, Jesus heals a blind man. After confirming the man's newfound sight and questioning him at length, the Pharisees blindly refuse to see that Jesus's words and deeds are from God. It is the man who was actually blind, on the other hand, who sees Jesus as the Son of Man and believes in him (John 9:38).

How did Jesus turn the tables on the Pharisees who considered themselves above the blind man, even to the point of reviling him and condemning him for being born in "utter sin"?

_____

_____

The Pharisees' spiritual blindness and inability to recognize Jesus at work, right before their eyes, kept them in darkness. The blind man's faith gave him true sight. The gift of physical sight that Jesus gave the blind man was an outward sign "to manifest the works of God" pointing to the gift of faith that allowed the man to truly see.

The Pharisee and Publican, unknown
© wikimedia.org

Blindness and darkness, then, signify the failure to recognize the work of Christ, who is the true "light of the world" (John 8:12) and the only one who can bring us out of darkness.

> *In Jesus Christ, the whole of God's truth has been made manifest. "Full of grace and truth," he came as the "light of the world," he is the Truth. "Whoever believes in me may not remain in darkness." The disciple of Jesus continues in his word so as to know "the truth [that] will make you free" and that sanctifies. To follow Jesus is to live in "the Spirit of truth," whom the Father sends in his name and who leads "into all the truth."*
> —*Catechism of the Catholic Church*, 2466

SESSION 9

NOT JUST FOR OTHER PEOPLE

Having the proper perspective on sin in our own lives is essential to no longer being blind and to allowing the light and truth of Christ to change us.

Jesus tells a parable that illustrates someone who *did not* consider his own sin. Read the parable in Luke 18:10–14 and answer the following questions. What was the focus of the Pharisee's prayer? What was the focus of the tax collector's prayer?

_____
_____
_____

According to Jesus, what do we need to do in order to receive justification like the tax collector?

_____
_____
_____

Humility allows us to recognize the sinful and dark areas in our hearts and to see Jesus as the light that will cast out that darkness. "A trusting humility brings us back into the light of communion between the Father and his Son Jesus Christ" (*CCC*, 2631). We must ask Christ to illuminate our minds and grant us the humility to ask forgiveness for the sins we have committed.

The *Catechism of the Catholic Church* teaches the value of *interiority*, of being "present to [oneself] in order to hear and follow the voice of [one's] conscience" (*CCC*, 1779). Interiority provides the opportunity for reflection, self-examination, and introspection as we take responsibility for the actions we have done and ask forgiveness for our sins (see *CCC*, 1779–1781).

How do the following passages encourage us to regularly examine our lowliness and practice humility before God?

Psalms 77:6: _____
_____

Isaiah 66:2: _____
_____

Philippians 2:3: _____
_____

As Dr. Barber teaches in the session, in order to feel the weight of Jesus's words, we must be careful to not misunderstand the Pharisees. Though Jesus uses them as examples of what *not* to do, it is not because they were all hypocrites concerned only with exterior righteousness. Many Pharisees were truly concerned with authentic righteousness. Jesus's use of them in many of his teachings on interior conversion illustrates that if *even* the Pharisees need to be purified in their hearts, how much more must we be vigilant against spiritual darkness.

Commit—Day 2
Harden Not Your Hearts

Throughout Scripture, man is reminded of his "heart problem." Our hearts are wounded by sin. Jesus offers us transformation through grace, but in order for us to be humble enough to receive his help, we must understand how seriously we are wounded. How does Jeremiah describe the problem of the human heart in the following passage?

Jeremiah 17:9: _____

_____

Our hearts are where we dwell in our innermost selves. It is where we choose to follow God or not follow him (*CCC*, 2563). So, when we find ourselves struggling with sin, it does not help us to blame external forces or to even excuse our actions by calling them mere "mistakes." Our choice came from us—from our heart—and when we firmly acknowledge that, we can, in humility, receive forgiveness and healing from God, who has promised to give us "a new heart" (Ezekiel 36:26).

What do the following passages say about recognizing our sins and admitting them openly to God?

Proverbs 28:13: _____

_____

Sirach 4:26: _____

_____

James 5:16: _____

_____

It is not always easy to take responsibility for our sins. Consider two examples from Scripture. Look up the following passages and note the responses of each of the people who sinned against God. Did these people blame others or themselves?

Adam and Eve (Genesis 3:8–13): _____

_____

Aaron and the Golden Calf (Exodus 32:21–24): _____

_____

King David also committed serious sin and was confronted about it by the prophet Nathan. When he realized his wrongdoing, how did David react?

David (2 Samuel 12:7–14): _____

_____

SESSION 9

Psalm 51 is said to have been composed by King David after his affair with Bathsheba and his murder of her husband. Read Psalm 51. What makes it a model prayer for all people when we sin?

_____

_____

This psalm also offers particular insight into the root causes of sin in our lives. Psalm 51:5 states, "Behold, I was brought forth in iniquity, and in sin did my mother conceive me." This passage teaches why we struggle with sin: we have a fallen human nature. When Adam and Eve rejected the gifts of God, among them were his gifts of original holiness and original justice as we discussed in session 5. As descendants of Adam and Eve, we lack a rightly ordered heart. (For more on this topic, see *CCC*, 402–206.)

Our fallen nature does not excuse our wrongdoings, but it does explain why we need a savior. Sin reigns in the world where death exists (see Romans 5:21), and we are enslaved to it without Christ (see Romans 6:6).

King David
© Zvonimir Atletic/shutterstock.com

> *The more one does what is good, the freer one becomes. There is no true freedom except in the service of what is good and just. The choice to disobey and do evil is an abuse of freedom and leads to "the slavery of sin."*
>
> —Catechism of the Catholic Church, 1733

We should recognize how readily we can be in denial about our own enslavement to sin. If we do not see our enslavement, we not only fail to seek and receive God's help, but we often feel offended at the suggestion that we are spiritually weak. We justify our sins or blame God for his moral laws that we mistakenly think are depriving us.

This has been the devil's trick from the beginning. The serpent planted seeds of doubt about God's goodness and generosity. He suggested to Adam and Eve that God was withholding something that would make them happy. Then man "let his trust in his Creator die in his heart" (*CCC*, 397), and when his wrongdoing was exposed, Adam hid himself because he was "afraid" (Genesis 3:10).

God is our Savior. He delivers us from our enslavement to sin. Let us not harden our heart and make the mistake of Adam, hiding ourselves in fear. But let us hear the words of David and confidently and humbly bring our brokenness to God, proclaiming with David, "[A] broken and a contrite heart, O God, you will not despise" (Psalm 51:17).

Commit—Day 3

Lectio: Seeing Clearly

As Jesus teaches his disciples, one theme repeatedly emerges: humility and the willingness to recognize our own shortcomings. In our *lectio* passage, Jesus provides us with a powerful illustration of the importance of not seeing ourselves as superior to others. Take some time to read, study, and pray on the following words of Christ.

> **Lectio:** The practice of praying with Scripture, *lectio divina* begins with an active and close reading of the Scripture passage. Read the verse below and then answer the questions to take a closer look at some of the details of the passage.

Why do you see the speck that is in your brother's eye, but do not notice the log that is in your own eye? Or how can you say to your brother, "Brother, let me take out the speck that is in your eye," when you yourself do not see the log that is in your own eye? You hypocrite, first take the log out of your own eye, and then you will see clearly to take out the speck that is in your brother's eye.

—Luke 6:41–42

How many times does this passage use the verb "see" or "notice"?
_____

The passage uses the verb "see" several times, but only once does it refer to "seeing clearly." What must we do to "see clearly"?
_____

What do you think Jesus is saying by using "speck" and "log"—two objects that are very different in size?
_____

A "hypocrite" can be defined as "an actor under an assumed character or a pretender." How does "acting" and "pretending" relate to what Jesus is saying here?
_____

Does this passage say that it is wrong to desire to remove the speck from another's eye?
_____

SESSION 9

> **MEDITATIO:** *Lectio*, a close reading and rereading of Scripture, is followed by *meditatio*, a time to reflect on the Scripture passage and to ponder the reason for particular events, descriptions, details, phrases, and even echoes from other Scripture passages that were noticed during *lectio*. Take some time now to meditate on the above verse.

The word **hypocrites** *in fact signifies pretenders. Hence, we ought especially to avoid that meddlesome class of pretenders who under the pretense of seeking advice undertake the censure of all kinds of vices. They are often moved by hatred and malice. Rather, whenever necessity compels one to reprove or rebuke another, we ought to proceed with godly discernment and caution. First of all, let us consider whether the other fault is such as we ourselves have never had or whether it is one that we have overcome. Then, if we have never had such a fault, let us remember that we are human and could have had it. But if we have had it and are rid of it now, let us remember our common frailty, in order that mercy, not hatred, may lead us to giving of correction and admonition. . . . But if on reflection we find that we ourselves have the same fault as the one we are about to reprove, let us neither correct nor rebuke that one. Rather, let us bemoan the fault of ourselves and induce that person to a similar concern, without asking him to submit to our correction.*

—St. Augustine, commentary on the Sermon on the Mount

Saints Augustine and Monica, Ary Scheffer
© commons.wikimedia.org

It is important to engage upon self-reflection before reproving a person for something we perceive as a sin or imperfection. According to St. Augustine, what is one of the first things we must avoid when correcting another?

_____

_____

SESSION 9

If we believe we must reprove another, and we do not believe we are moved by hatred or malice but a sincere love for the other, we have to examine ourselves and our own past. What does Augustine teach that we should do if we have not struggled with the particular fault that we feel we should reprove?

_____
_____

What should we do if we discern that we are currently struggling with the same fault as our brother or sister and have not yet conquered it?

_____
_____

How does this approach to self-reflection and honesty with our own weakness put into practice the teachings of Jesus regarding the Pharisee and the tax collector in Luke 18:10–14?

_____
_____

What are tangible steps you can take to practice examining weakness in your life?

_____
_____

> *Examine yourself: slowly, courageously. Is it not true that your bad humour and your gloominess, both without cause—without apparent cause—are due to your lack of determination in breaking the subtle but real snares laid for you—cunningly and attractively—by your concupiscence?*
> —St. Josemaria Escrivá, *The Way*, 237

> ### ORATIO, CONTEMPLATIO, RESOLUTIO:
> Having read and meditated on today's Scripture passage, take some time to pray, to bring your thoughts to God (*oratio*), and to be receptive to God's grace in silence (*contemplatio*). Then end your prayer by making a simple concrete resolution (*resolutio*) to respond to God's prompting of your heart in today's prayer.

_____
_____
_____

Commit–Day 4
The Need for Supernatural Vision

The gift of salvation God offers to mankind is so generous that those who heard Jesus had a difficult time understanding and believing him. How do the following passages demonstrate that the disciples had a difficult time wrapping their minds around what Jesus was teaching?

Luke 18:34: _____

_____

John 6:56–61: _____

_____

The Descent from the Cross, Peter Paul Rubens
© commons.wikimedia.org

Nicodemus is another example of a person who could not see the gift Jesus was offering and instead saw Jesus's words in earthly terms. Dr. Barber explains that Jesus tells Nicodemus that man needs to be "born *anothen*." Jesus uses a Greek word that can have two meanings. It could either mean "again" or "from above." When Jesus spoke of being "born *anothen*," it seemed more likely to Nicodemus that Jesus was suggesting a person enter his mother's womb for a second time rather than thinking Jesus meant that we must be born "from above."

SESSION 9 — NOT JUST FOR OTHER PEOPLE

Like Nicodemus, we need God's help to understand, to have a supernatural vision of things "from above." It is God's gift of faith that enables us to see Jesus's words and understand them correctly. As the *Catechism of the Catholic Church* states, "Believing is possible only by grace and the interior helps of the Holy Spirit. But it is no less true that believing is an authentically human act. Trusting in God and cleaving to the truths he has revealed is contrary neither to human freedom nor to human reason" (*CCC*, 154).

Allegory of Faith, Francesco Fontebasso
© commons.wikimedia.org

Faith is a gift of God, but it also requires our participation, cooperation, and willingness to trust in God, who has demonstrated that he is trustworthy through his signs and wonders in salvation history, in the life of Christ, and in the lives of the saints (*CCC*, 156). Faith requires trusting in God and humbling ourselves in light of his greater plan—a plan that our limited vision often cannot correctly understand right away. Faith is not intended to be a "blind leap," as many people use the phrase today. What do the following passages say about faith, and how does that connect with what God has done to establish our trust?

Hebrews 11:1: _____

_____

James 1:5–6: _____

_____

Faith also requires us to depend on others and trust God to speak and work even through imperfect people. No one hears the Gospel by himself; no one can baptize himself. The gift of faith comes to us from God through other people. As the *Catechism of the Catholic Church* teaches, "No one can believe alone" (*CCC*, 166). We receive the faith from others who tell us about God, and, in turn, we are called to be "a link in the great chain of believers" (*CCC*, 166) and speak to others about the faith.

Scripture speaks of the importance of developing friendships that "encourage one another" (1 Thessalonians 5:11). Humbly recognizing that we can be susceptible to spiritual blindness, we should seek out friends who are not "blind guides" but people who help us see clearly with a supernatural vision.

When David sinned, God spoke through the prophet Nathan to convict David of his sinfulness, which led to David's repentance. Think about how the income might have been different if Nathan did not have the courage and wisdom from God to confront David and speak the truth to him.

In our own lives, we also need friends who love God and who love us enough to help us avoid sin. St. Francis de Sales speaks about the gift of these sorts of friends:

> *"A faithful friend," we are told in Holy Scripture, "is a sturdy shelter: he that has found one has found a treasure" (Sir 6:14); and again: "A faithful friend is an elixir of life; and those who fear the Lord will find him" (Sir 6:16). These sacred words have chiefly reference, as you see, to the immortal life, with a view to which we specially need a faithful friend, who will guide us by his counsel and advice, thereby guarding us against the deceits and snares of the Evil One—he will be as a storehouse of wisdom to us in our sorrows, trials and falls; he will be as a healing balm to stay and soothe our heart in the time of spiritual sickness—he will shield us from evil, and confirm that which is good in us, and when we fall through infirmity, he will avert the deadly nature of the evil, and raise us up again. But who can find such a friend? The wise man answers: "The man who fears the Lord" (Sir 15:1): that is to say, the truly humble soul that earnestly desires to advance in the spiritual life.*

Saint Francis de Sales Oratory
(St. Louis, Missouri)
© Wikicommons.com

St. Paul recognized the value of looking out for each other in the spiritual life. What does he say in the following passages that demonstrates how we are called to assist each other in living for Christ and avoiding sin?

1 Corinthians 4:14–16: _____

Colossians 3:16: _____

1 Thessalonians 5:14: _____

> *The virtuous soul that is alone and without a master is like a burning coal; it will grow colder rather than hotter.*
> —St. John of the Cross,
> "The Sayings of Light and Love"

John of the Cross, Francisco de Zurbarán
© commons.wikimedia.org

COMMIT–DAY 5
TRUTH AND BEAUTY

Jesus Opens Eyes of a Man Born Blind
Duccio di Buoninsegna, 1311, National Gallery, London

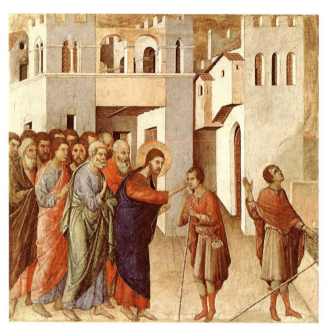

Jesus Opens Eyes of a Man Born Blind, Duccio di Buoninsegna
© commons.wikimedia.org

Duccio di Buoninsegna was one of the great medieval painters of Sienna. His greatest work is known as the Maestà Altarpiece, which was completed in the early 1300s for the Sienna Cathedral. The principle image on the front of this magnificent work was of the Madonna and Child enthroned, with a series of small images of the childhood of Christ running along the predella, along the frame at the bottom of the altarpiece. The back of the altarpiece was also painted and contained over forty small images depicting scenes from the life of the Virgin and the life of Christ. *Jesus Opens Eyes of a Man Born Blind* was one of the predella paintings depicting the life of Christ on the back side of the altarpiece.

At the center of this painting, Christ heals the blind man. Christ gently leans forward to anoint the man's eyes with mud. The blind man's helplessness is emphasized by his darkened eyes, his upraised hand, and his walking stick. He cannot see Jesus, but he raises his hand, perhaps to feel the hand of Christ that reaches out to touch him.

SESSION 9

NOT JUST FOR OTHER PEOPLE

The blind man is dressed in garments of simple earthen tones. In contrast, Christ is dressed in bright red and blue trimmed with gold. In the tradition of Byzantine icons, which many medieval painters continued, red and blue were used to represent Christ's two natures, human and divine, thus recalling how at his Incarnation Jesus assumed our human nature, becoming truly man while remaining truly God. Duccio emphasizes Christ's divine nature by surrounding his sacred head with a gold halo. Christ, the radiant Son of God, comes to bring light to the humble blind man, the blind man who previously could not see and could only feel his way with his walking stick.

Closely behind Jesus follow his Twelve Apostles. Jesus and the Apostles are in Jerusalem for the Feast of Tabernacles (John 7:10) and have just left the Temple, when they pass by a man born blind. The three disciples closest to Jesus, likely Peter (with his curly, gray hair), James, and John (with his youthful face), are clothed in bright colors, probably due to their proximity to Christ (recall these are the three Apostles who will be bathed in the glorious light of Christ's Transfiguration). In the background of the painting stand the buildings of the city, with their myriad of doors, windows, arches, and pillars. The simple gold background of Byzantine images is being pushed to the periphery and in its place stands the more natural city familiar to the painting's viewer.

One of the striking elements of this painting is the medieval convention of displaying multiple scenes from the story in the same image. This painting is not a snapshot of one moment in time. Rather, Duccio depicts the blind man both being healed and praising God after he is healed. To the right of the blind man and Christ, the blind man is depicted again. The second depiction shows him when his sight is restored, eyes wide open looking heavenward after washing in the pool of Siloam. Appearing at the edge of the painting to the right of the healed blind man, the pool is depicted as a medieval city fountain.

Now seeing, the blind man raises his hand in praise of God. He was hunched over, but now stands upright. He drops the walking stick, previously essential to his survival. He abandons the tool he created for himself in favor of the clear sight of Christ. Look up John 9:35–41. How does the blind man express his faith? How does Duccio represent the blind man's faith?

_____

_____

_____

In the original altarpiece, the painting just to the right of Duccio's *Jesus Opens Eyes of a Man Born Blind* was *The Transfiguration* of Christ. Thus, the blind man in *Jesus Opens Eyes of a Man Born Blind*, after receiving Christ's healing power, would have appeared to be gazing at the transfigured Christ in the next panel. Like the blind man, our surest cure for spiritual blindness is to keep our eyes on Christ.

SESSION 9

Take a moment to journal your ideas, questions, or insights about this session. Write down thoughts you had that may not have been mentioned in the text or the discussion questions. List any personal applications you got from the lessons. What challenged you the most in the teachings? How might you turn what you've learned into specific action?

SESSION 10

Not Only about the Future

OPENING PRAYER

Lord Jesus, our Redeemer,
you willingly gave yourself up to death,
so that all might be saved and pass from death to life.
You alone are the Holy One, you are mercy itself;
by dying you unlocked the gates of life for those who believe in you.
Forgive our sins,
and grant us a place of happiness, light, and peace
in the kingdom of your glory for ever and ever.
Amen.
—Adapted from the Concluding Prayer from the Order of Christian Funerals

INTRODUCTION

Why is it so hard to avoid temptation? In this session, we'll look at Scripture passages that remind us we are not alone (since all creation is struggling) and that give us remedies to strengthen us to win the battle against temptation. The new creation is not merely about the future, but can enter our lives here and now. Let's find out how!

© Andre Gie/shutterstock.com

Connect

Have you ever attempted a new exercise regimen or diet? Was it difficult to begin? Was it difficult to continue? Describe your experience.

Do you practice particular disciplines in the season of Lent? What is your experience trying to keep the resolutions you set? Do you feel keeping the resolutions benefits your spiritual life?

 ## Video
Watch the video segment. Use the outline below to follow along and take notes.

I. Salvation and Resurrection
   A. God saves us body and soul
      1. Christian worldview values the body
      2. Secular worldview sees body as merely something that will die
   B. New creation is not just a distant reality (1 Corinthians 15:20–22; 2 Corinthians 5:17)
   C. Old creation
      1. Adam's sin affected all humanity (Romans 5:12)
      2. Sin disordered our intellect, will, and desires (Romans 7:19)
   D. Triple concupiscence
      1. Summary of all sins in three categories (1 John 2:16)
         a. Lust of the flesh, pleasures of the senses
         b. Lust of the eyes, covetousness of earthly goods
         c. Pride of life, self-assertion
      2. Present in Original Sin
      3. Christ, the New Adam, overcomes these temptations (*CCC*, 538)

SESSION 10

II. New creation in Christ
   A. Remedy for triple concupiscence (Matthew 6)
      1. Fasting
      2. Almsgiving
      3. Prayer
   B. Conformity to God's will even in suffering
      1. "Not my will but your will be done"
      2. Share in the Resurrection of Christ

Discuss

1. What was something in the lecture that was new to you?

2. Why is it important to understand that salvation pertains to our bodies as well as our souls?

3. What is the "triple concupiscence" and how does it relate to Adam and Eve? How does the triple concupiscence relate to sins we commit in our lives today?

4. What should our response be when we encounter God not answering our prayers as we would hope? How do we remain faithful in suffering?

SESSION 10

NOT ONLY ABOUT THE FUTURE

QUOTES, TIPS, & DEFINITIONS

CONCUPISCENCE

The movement of the sensitive appetite contrary to the operation of the human reason.
—Catechism of the Catholic Church, 2515

ASCESIS

The practice of penance, mortification, and self-denial to promote greater self-mastery and to foster the way of perfection by embracing the way of the cross.
—Catechism of the Catholic Church, Glossary

MEMORY VERSE

Therefore, if any one is in Christ, he is a new creation; the old has passed away, behold, the new has come.
—2 Corinthians 5:17

CLOSING PRAYER

Praised be my Lord for our sister, the death of the body,
from which no one escapes.
Woe to him who dies in mortal sin!
Blessed are they who are found walking by your most holy will,
for the second death shall have no power to do them harm.
Praise you, and bless you the Lord,
and give thanks to God, and serve God with great humility.
—Excerpt from St. Francis of Assisi's "Canticle of the Sun"

FOR FURTHER READING

Joseph Cardinal Ratzinger, *Spirit of the Liturgy* (San Francisco: Ignatius Press, 2000)

Pitre, Barber, Kincaid, "Paul and Apocalyptic" and "New Covenant Justification through Divine Sonship," *Paul, a New Covenant Jew: Rethinking Pauline Theology* (Grand Rapids: Eerdmans, 2019)

Pope Benedict XVI, Encyclical Letter, *Caritas in Veritate*

Commit—Day 1
The Resurrection and a New Creation

© VRstudio/shutterstock.com

When Adam and Eve disobeyed God, they wounded their relationship with God and each other, as well as the integrity within themselves. They also destroyed the harmony they enjoyed with creation. Before sin, man had dominion over creation (Genesis 1:26) and was even tasked with naming all living creatures, demonstrating his cooperation with God's providence (Genesis 2:19; see *CCC*, 373). What do the following passages reveal about the relationship between man and creation after sin?

Genesis 3:17–19: _____

_____

Romans 8:21: _____

_____

We know that, in his Death and Resurrection Jesus reverses the effects of sin and death for humanity. We share in this victory when we are united to Christ. Scripture reveals that Christ's redemption also involves reversing the damage that sin caused between man and creation. What does Scripture say about creation now as it battles with the consequences of sin?

Galatians 1:3–5: _____

_____

1 Corinthians 7:31: _____

_____

SESSION 10

Not Only about the Future

What does Scripture say about the future of creation once it shares in Christ's redemption?

2 Corinthians 5:17: _____

_____

Isaiah 66:22: _____

_____

When Adam sinned, all creation suffered from his downfall. In Christ's work of redemption, all creation shares in Jesus's glory. In Adam, death was ushered into the world. In Christ, through his Resurrection, new life is given. This life refers not only to the spiritual life he gives through grace but also to a healing of the *material* world. Jesus passed through death and was resurrected with a glorified body. His glorified body was a real body, and it was certainly changed.

Resurrection of Christ, Juan Correa de Vivar
© commons.wikimedia.org

Look up the following passages. What evidence do we see that Christ's resurrected body was material and that he was not only a spirit?

Luke 24:39: _____

_____

John 20:27–28: _____

_____

SESSION 10

Not Only about the Future

Doubting Thomas with St. Magnus, Cima da Conegliano
© wikiart.org

We have seen that Jesus's body was similar to his pre-Resurrection body in that he ate food and that people were able to touch him. What does Scripture say about how his body was different after his Resurrection?

Luke 24:31: _____
_____

John 20:19: _____
_____

Jesus's resurrected body is no longer subject to death. St. Paul teaches that those who are united to Christ in his Death will share in his Resurrection: "When the perishable puts on the imperishable, and the mortal puts on immortality, then shall come to pass the saying that is written: 'Death is swallowed up in victory'" (1 Corinthians 15:54).

SESSION 10   NOT ONLY ABOUT THE FUTURE

The Woman with an Issue of Blood,
James Tissot
© Brooklyn Museum/
commons.wikimedia.org

Since all creation suffered in the Fall of Adam and Eve, so too all creation is given redemption in Jesus.

The fracturing of the harmony between man and creation will be healed. We begin to see this in Christ's own work in his earthly ministry. While Jesus was able to heal simply with a word of command (as with the centurion's servant in Matthew 8:8), Jesus often used the material world as instruments of his healing. What did Jesus use in each of the following passages to accomplish his saving work?

Mark 5:25–29: _____

_____

John 9:5–6: _____

_____

Mark 8:22–26: _____

_____

After his Death and Resurrection, Jesus instructs his apostles to carry out his saving work and to use the created world to communicate *supernatural* grace to us. His apostles use water to baptize and bread and wine made from grain and grapes, respectively, to give us eternal life in the Eucharist (see John 6). The material world plays an important role in the work of redemption, and it too will be redeemed and set free from the effects of sin in the new creation.

Commit—Day 2
Resurrection and New Life

The new creation in Christ is something that will be perfected at the end of time, but it has already been inaugurated with the Resurrection of Jesus (*CCC*, 2190). How is this "new creation" accomplished in us as we strive to be conformed to Christ? Let's begin by looking at Romans 8:23. According to St. Paul, what indication is there that the redemption of our bodies is not necessarily going to be easy?

_____
_____

Our bodies have been affected by the reign of sin and it will take effort to put the desires of the flesh into right order with our reason and our will. When we experience a physical desire, such as for food or comfort, it can be consuming. In some cases, we make choices that we know are not good choices, but we choose those things because they bring our body pleasure, comfort, or satisfaction. We experience this when we eat food that is not good for us, simply because we enjoy its flavor. Our body wanted it, and despite knowing that we probably should not eat it, we could not resist the physical desire.

St. Paul speaks a great deal about the dangers of living by the "flesh." What warnings do the following passages give us?

Romans 8:5–8: _____
_____
_____

1 Corinthians 15:50: _____
_____
_____

Galatians 5:17: _____
_____
_____

This is not to say that the body is bad. When Paul speaks about the "flesh," it is distinct from when he speaks about the body. His emphasis on the flesh focuses on our disordered desires. We recognize that our bodies are subject to sin and need redemption in order to be conformed to the glory of Christ's body. This transformation of our bodies and the ordering of our desires begins with God's saving grace at Baptism, but it will take effort and struggle to fully achieve.

© Mladen Zivkovic/shutterstock.com

The analogy that New Testament writers often use to describe the discipline required to put the desires of the flesh back under the reign of right reason is that of an athlete training for a competition. Look up the following passages and note what Paul says about what we can learn from athletes:

1 Corinthians 9:25: _____

_____

1 Timothy 4:7–8: _____

_____

Hebrews 12:11: _____

_____

Similar to an athlete who must train his or her muscles for the skills and habits of a particular sport, we must form our conscience according to the Word of God and the Church's teachings, and train our wills to exercise control over our bodies so as to avoid sin. And just as an athlete exercises daily to be ready for a competition, we should exercise and strengthen our will's control over our desires with small daily sacrifices, penances, and mortifications. Denying our flesh its temporal desires strengthens our will so that when faced with an occasion of sin we have the will to victoriously overcome temptation.

SESSION 10

NOT ONLY ABOUT THE FUTURE

© Vasyl Shulga/shutterstock.com

St. John Paul II reiterated St. Paul's teaching as he spoke to the athletes of the Bologna soccer team in 1978:

> [B]ut you young sportsmen have a special place, because you offer, in a preeminent way, a spectacle of fortitude, loyalty and self-control, and also because you have to a marked extent the sense of honour, friendship and brotherly solidarity: virtues which the Church promotes and exalts. Continue, dear young men, to give the best of yourselves in sports competitions, always remembering that the competitive spirit of the sportsman, though so noble in itself, must not be an end in itself, but must be subordinated to the far more noble requirements of the spirit. Therefore, while I repeat to you: be good sportsmen, I also say to you: be good citizens in family and social life, and, even more, be good Christians, who are able to give a superior meaning to life, in such a way as to be able to put into practice what the Apostle Paul said about athletes to Christians of his time: "Do you not know that in a race all the runners compete, but only one receives the prize? So run that you may obtain it . . . They (athletes) do it to receive a perishable wreath, but we an imperishable" (1 Cor 9:24–25).

St. Paul speaks about taking "pains [in Greek, *ascesis*] to have a clear conscience toward God and toward men" (Acts 24:16). From this starting point, the Church has developed a rich understanding of ascetical theology: whereby we make use of physical penances to progress in the spiritual life. Our willingness to "take pains" and make use of certain practices of self-denial strengthens our will so that we can respond more fully to God's grace and progress along the road of perfection. Willingly denying our bodies comfort and pleasure strengthens our will to more readily respond to God's will, changing our desires for earthly goods into a growing desire for God himself.

What are some ways you can practice self-denial to strengthen your will to help bring about Christ's victory over sin and the dawn of the new creation in your life?

_____

_____

Commit—Day 3
Lectio: Christ Has Been Raised

St. Paul writes to the Christians at Corinth, some of whom are wrestling with doubt about Christ's Resurrection. At times, it can be difficult for us to truly have faith in those things that we cannot yet see. As we wrestle with our own imperfections and the places in our hearts that are not yet conformed to Christ, we can doubt that we will ever gain the upper hand over sin and death. Let's turn to St. Paul's words and meditate on the conviction with which he speaks about his faith in the Resurrection of Christ.

> **Lectio:** The practice of praying with Scripture, *lectio divina* begins with an active and close reading of the Scripture passage. Read the verse below and then answer the questions to take a closer look at some of the details of the passage.

Now if Christ is preached as raised from the dead, how can some of you say that there is no resurrection of the dead? But if there is no resurrection of the dead, then Christ has not been raised; if Christ has not been raised, then our preaching is in vain and your faith is in vain. We are even found to be misrepresenting God, because we testified of God that he raised Christ, whom he did not raise if it is true that the dead are not raised. For if the dead are not raised, then Christ has not been raised. If Christ has not been raised, your faith is futile and you are still in your sins. Then those also who have fallen asleep in Christ have perished. If for this life only we have hoped in Christ, we are of all men most to be pitied. But in fact Christ has been raised from the dead, the first fruits of those who have fallen asleep. For as by a man came death, by a man has come also the resurrection of the dead. For as in Adam all die, so also in Christ shall all be made alive.

—1 Corinthians 15:12–22

What seems to be the concern St. Paul is addressing in the opening sentence? What are some members of the Church of Corinth saying about Jesus's Resurrection?

_____
_____
_____

How many times does Paul refer to being "raised" or to "resurrection"?

_____
_____
_____

SESSION 10

Not Only about the Future

St. Paul leads his audience through a series of "If . . . then" statements regarding Jesus's Resurrection. What is the consequence if Christ has not been raised from the dead?

_____

_____

After the series of "If . . . then" statements, what does St. Paul emphatically declare with the words "But in fact . . ."?

_____

_____

> **MEDITATIO:** *Lectio*, a close reading and rereading of Scripture, is followed by *meditatio*, a time to reflect on the Scripture passage and to ponder the reason for particular events, descriptions, details, phrases, and even echoes from other Scripture passages that were noticed during *lectio*. Take some time now to meditate on the above verse.

Resurrection of Christ, Giovanni Bellini
© wikiart.org

SESSION 10

NOT ONLY ABOUT THE FUTURE

The Resurrection of Jesus is the fundamental event upon which Christian faith rests (cf. 1 Cor 15:14). It is an astonishing reality, fully grasped in the light of faith, yet historically attested to by those who were privileged to see the Risen Lord. It is a wondrous event which is not only absolutely unique in human history, but which lies at the very heart of the mystery of time. In fact, "all time belongs to [Christ] and all the ages"; as the evocative liturgy of the Easter Vigil recalls in preparing the Paschal Candle. Therefore, in commemorating the day of Christ's Resurrection not just once a year but every Sunday, the Church seeks to indicate to every generation the true fulcrum of history, to which the mystery of the world's origin and its final destiny leads.

— St. John Paul II

For St. Paul, to encounter people at Corinth who doubted Jesus's Resurrection seemed unthinkable! If Christ did not rise from the dead, then nothing he said or did makes sense. The restoration of life to mankind and the redemption of our flesh is what makes sense of the entire purpose of salvation history and gives meaning to our lives.

How do you think it affects a person to go through life having no hope in the resurrection and in the redemption of the body, and instead believing once he or she died, there was nothing after death?

_____
_____

The Holy Father describes the Resurrection as the "fulcrum of history." What does he mean that the Resurrection is that to which the "mystery of the world's origin and its final destiny leads"?

_____
_____

The Holy Father speaks of the Resurrection as "an astonishing reality" and a "wondrous event." Take some time today to meditate on the Resurrection and to praise and thank God for this wondrous event.

> **ORATIO, CONTEMPLATIO, RESOLUTIO:** Having read and meditated on today's Scripture passage, take some time to pray, to bring your thoughts to God (*oratio*), and to be receptive to God's grace in silence (*contemplatio*). Then end your prayer by making a simple concrete resolution (*resolutio*) to respond to God's prompting of your heart in today's prayer.

_____
_____

Commit—Day 4
Sharing in the New Adam's Victory over Satan

St. Augustine says that Original Sin "embraces all sins." In the sin of Adam and Eve, we can see our own struggles.

Read 1 John 2:16. What three things does this passage say are "in the world"?

___

___

Christ in the Wilderness, Ivan Kramskoi
© commons.wikimedia.org

The lust of the flesh, the lust of the eyes, and the pride of life are three categories into which any sin can be placed. When we sin, we are falling prey to one of these temptations. If our sin involves gluttony, laziness, or seeking some physical pleasure, those sins are according to the lust of the flesh. If we are desirous of riches and wealth and we commit sin to accumulate money and material possessions, then we have succumbed to the lust of the eyes. If we commit sin in order to elevate ourselves in others' esteem or to raise our status, then we are guilty of the pride of life.

SESSION 10

Let's examine how the forbidden fruit tempted Adam and Eve to renounce their life with God. Fill in the third column of the table by consulting Genesis 3:6.

The Threefold Lust (1 John 2:16)	Three Temptations	The Forbidden Fruit (Genesis 3:6)
"the lust of the flesh"	"pleasure of the senses"	
"the lust of the eyes"	"covetousness of earthly goods"	
"the pride of life"	"self-assertion"	

Jesus took on the debt humanity incurred by its infidelity to God. In the desert, Jesus overcame the three temptations of Adam and Eve. Let's look at the temptation narrative to see the significance of the temptations Jesus overcame in relation to the temptations Adam and Eve failed to overcome. Read the following passages and describe the temptation Jesus faced.

First Temptation—Matthew 4:3: _____

_____

Second Temptation—Matthew 4:6: _____

_____

Third Temptation—Matthew 4:8–9: _____

_____

How do these correspond to the threefold lusts and the temptations faced by Adam and Eve?

The Threefold Lust (1 John 2:16)	Three Temptations	The Forbidden Fruit (Genesis 3:6)	Jesus's Temptations
"the lust of the flesh"	"pleasure of the senses"	"good for food"	
"the lust of the eyes"	"covetousness of earthly goods"	"delight to the eyes"	
"the pride of life"	"self-assertion"	desirable "to make one wise"	

SESSION 10

NOT ONLY ABOUT THE FUTURE

© GotovyyStock/shutterstock.com

Jesus gives us specific teachings so that we can enjoy freedom from sin and have victory over the threefold concupiscence. Look at the following passages from the Sermon on the Mount. What disciplines does Jesus presuppose that his disciples will practice?

Matthew 6:16-17: _____

Matthew 6:3-4: _____

Matthew 6:5-6: _____

Fill in the table below with the corresponding disciplines of fasting, almsgiving, and prayer, which are taught by Christ as remedies to our concupiscence:

The Threefold Lust (1 John 2:16)	Three Temptations	The Forbidden Fruit (Genesis 3:6)	Jesus's Temptations	Three Spiritual Disciplines
"the lust of the flesh"	"pleasure of the senses"	"good for food"	satisfy hunger	
"the lust of the eyes"	"covetousness of earthly goods"	"delight to the eyes"	receive the glory of the kingdoms	
"the pride of life"	"self-assertion"	desirable "to make one wise"	call upon angelic intervention	

By fasting, we deny the body the pleasures of food in order to develop the habit of denying our body other pleasures it desires—pleasures that may be sinful. By almsgiving, we renounce our love for riches and place trust in God to provide for our needs. By prayer, we recognize our dependence on God and reject a prideful trust in ourselves. If we diligently act on God's grace and put these disciplines into practice, we will experience God's salvation at an ever-deepening level in our lives here and now.

COMMIT—DAY 5
TRUTH AND BEAUTY

The Resurrection
Pietro Novelli (1603–1647), unknown date, Prado Museum, Madrid, Spain

The Resurrection of Jesus Christ, Pietro Novelli
© restoredtraditions.com

Pietro Novelli, nicknamed "the Raphael of Sicily," was an Italian artist during the Baroque period. Novelli initially trained under his father, Pietro Antonio Novelli, who died in 1625 from the Black Death. Novelli's *The Resurrection* is not merely an exercise in foreshortening and dramatic arrangement but is a presentation of hope—the hope that those who had succumbed to a putrid death would one day rise whole and glorious to share in Christ's life.

The painting expresses the vitality of the Resurrection by capturing the very moment that Christ rose from the tomb. In this life-size painting (measuring nearly five feet by six feet), we see Jesus, the conqueror of death, emerging from the darkness of the grave, his right foot stepping on the edge of the tomb. Jesus's body is luminous, reflecting a heavenly light.

Not only do we see Christ triumphant in Novelli's painting, but we also seem to be seen *by* him. Jesus's penetrating gaze is the most striking thing in the painting. By a masterful use of line and color, Novelli forces us to "look upon him whom [we] have pierced" (John 19:37; see Zechariah 12:10) and to confront his eyes. We look at Jesus and he looks solemnly out at us—his eyes wide open to our reality.

Thus, while the tableau is glorious and triumphant, it is not joyful. Christ's face is solemn. He has conquered sin and death and now looks at the viewer, inviting us to pick up our cross and follow him and urging us to conquer ourselves with his grace. Facing Christ, how will you respond? Take a few minutes to consider if your life is truly arranged to help you conquer sin.

_____

_____

Return your gaze to the painting. After being transfixed by the eyes of Christ, the parallel lines of Christ's eyes and shoulders draw our attention to the top left of the work. There, Christ's right hand is raised in blessing. With this gesture, Christ indicates that we do not have to fight alone. He is with us; his grace is enough.

Lastly, turn your attention to the surrounding angels. While peripheral to the composition, their eyes all focus on Christ. You can trace each angel's line of sight to the face, hands, feet, and side of Christ. Though risen, Christ bears the marks of his Passion. The same will be true of us. The body with which we experience the world is the body we will have for all eternity. We should be diligent in following St. Paul's advice to "glorify God in your body" (1 Corinthians 6:20) here on earth so that our body will be glorified by God for all eternity.

The reality of Christ's Resurrection and its implications for our lives are as relevant now as ever. As St. Paul reminds us later in 1 Corinthians, "But in fact Christ has been raised from the dead" (1 Corinthians 15:20). He is the first fruits, so let us "be steadfast, immovable, always abounding in the work of the Lord" (1 Corinthians 15:58).

Take a moment to journal your ideas, questions, or insights about this session. Write down thoughts you had that may not have been mentioned in the text or the discussion questions. List any personal applications you got from the lessons. What challenged you the most in the teachings? How might you turn what you've learned into specific action?

_____

_____

_____

_____

_____

_____